Llewellyn's

Witches' Datebook

2005

Featuring

*Art by Jennifer Hewitson. Text by Elizabeth Barrette,
Gerina Dunwich, Ellen Dugan, Emely Flak,
Magenta Griffith, James Kambos, Edain McCoy,
ShadowCat, and Julianna Yau*

ISBN 0-7387-0142-4

2005

```
        JANUARY                FEBRUARY                 MARCH                   APRIL
 S  M  T  W  T  F  S     S  M  T  W  T  F  S     S  M  T  W  T  F  S     S  M  T  W  T  F  S
                    1              1  2  3  4  5              1  2  3  4  5                 1  2
 2  3  4  5  6  7  8     6  7  8  9 10 11 12     6  7  8  9 10 11 12     3  4  5  6  7  8  9
 9 10 11 12 13 14 15    13 14 15 16 17 18 19    13 14 15 16 17 18 19    10 11 12 13 14 15 16
16 17 18 19 20 21 22    20 21 22 23 24 25 26    20 21 22 23 24 25 26    17 18 19 20 21 22 23
23 24 25 26 27 28 29    27 28                   27 28 29 30 31          24 25 26 27 28 29 30
30 31

          MAY                    JUNE                    JULY                   AUGUST
 S  M  T  W  T  F  S     S  M  T  W  T  F  S     S  M  T  W  T  F  S     S  M  T  W  T  F  S
 1  2  3  4  5  6  7              1  2  3  4                    1  2        1  2  3  4  5  6
 8  9 10 11 12 13 14     5  6  7  8  9 10 11     3  4  5  6  7  8  9     7  8  9 10 11 12 13
15 16 17 18 19 20 21    12 13 14 15 16 17 18    10 11 12 13 14 15 16    14 15 16 17 18 19 20
22 23 24 25 26 27 28    19 20 21 22 23 24 25    17 18 19 20 21 22 23    21 22 23 24 25 26 27
29 30 31                26 27 28 29 30          24 25 26 27 28 29 30    28 29 30 31
                                                31

       SEPTEMBER               OCTOBER                NOVEMBER                DECEMBER
 S  M  T  W  T  F  S     S  M  T  W  T  F  S     S  M  T  W  T  F  S     S  M  T  W  T  F  S
             1  2  3                       1        1  2  3  4  5                    1  2  3
 4  5  6  7  8  9 10     2  3  4  5  6  7  8     6  7  8  9 10 11 12     4  5  6  7  8  9 10
11 12 13 14 15 16 17     9 10 11 12 13 14 15    13 14 15 16 17 18 19    11 12 13 14 15 16 17
18 19 20 21 22 23 24    16 17 18 19 20 21 22    20 21 22 23 24 25 26    18 19 20 21 22 23 24
25 26 27 28 29 30       23 24 25 26 27 28 29    27 28 29 30             25 26 27 28 29 30 31
                        30 31
```

2006

```
        JANUARY                FEBRUARY                 MARCH                   APRIL
 S  M  T  W  T  F  S     S  M  T  W  T  F  S     S  M  T  W  T  F  S     S  M  T  W  T  F  S
 1  2  3  4  5  6  7              1  2  3  4              1  2  3  4                       1
 8  9 10 11 12 13 14     5  6  7  8  9 10 11     5  6  7  8  9 10 11     2  3  4  5  6  7  8
15 16 17 18 19 20 21    12 13 14 15 16 17 18    12 13 14 15 16 17 18     9 10 11 12 13 14 15
22 23 24 25 26 27 28    19 20 21 22 23 24 25    19 20 21 22 23 24 25    16 17 18 19 20 21 22
29 30 31                26 27 28                26 27 28 29 30 31       23 24 25 26 27 28 29
                                                                        30

          MAY                    JUNE                    JULY                   AUGUST
 S  M  T  W  T  F  S     S  M  T  W  T  F  S     S  M  T  W  T  F  S     S  M  T  W  T  F  S
    1  2  3  4  5  6                 1  2  3                       1        1  2  3  4  5
 7  8  9 10 11 12 13     4  5  6  7  8  9 10     2  3  4  5  6  7  8     6  7  8  9 10 11 12
14 15 16 17 18 19 20    11 12 13 14 15 16 17     9 10 11 12 13 14 15    13 14 15 16 17 18 19
21 22 23 24 25 26 27    18 19 20 21 22 23 24    16 17 18 19 20 21 22    20 21 22 23 24 25 26
28 29 30 31             25 26 27 28 29 30       23 24 25 26 27 28 29    27 28 29 30 31
                                                30 31

       SEPTEMBER               OCTOBER                NOVEMBER                DECEMBER
 S  M  T  W  T  F  S     S  M  T  W  T  F  S     S  M  T  W  T  F  S     S  M  T  W  T  F  S
                1  2     1  2  3  4  5  6  7           1  2  3  4                    1  2
 3  4  5  6  7  8  9     8  9 10 11 12 13 14     5  6  7  8  9 10 11     3  4  5  6  7  8  9
10 11 12 13 14 15 16    15 16 17 18 19 20 21    12 13 14 15 16 17 18    10 11 12 13 14 15 16
17 18 19 20 21 22 23    22 23 24 25 26 27 28    19 20 21 22 23 24 25    17 18 19 20 21 22 23
24 25 26 27 28 29 30    29 30 31                26 27 28 29 30          24 25 26 27 28 29 30
                                                                        31
```

Editing/design by K. M. Brielmaier

Cover illustration and interior art © 2004 by Jennifer Hewitson

Art on chapter openings © 2004 by Kathleen Edwards

Cover design by Anne Marie Garrison

Art direction by Lynne Menturweck

Moon sign and phase data by Astro Communications Services

Table of Contents

How to Use Llewellyn's *Witches' Datebook*

W elcome to Llewellyn's *Witches' Datebook 2005*. This datebook was designed especially for Witches, Pagans, and magical people. Use it to plan sabbat celebrations, magic, Full Moon rites, and even dentist and doctor appointments! Below is a symbol key to some of the features of this datebook.

MOON QUARTERS: The Moon's cycle is divided into four quarters, which are noted in the calendar pages along with their exact times. When the Moon changes quarter, both quarters are listed, as well as the time of the change. In addition, a symbol for the new quarter is placed where the numeral for the date usually appears.

MOON IN THE SIGNS: Approximately every two and a half days the Moon moves from one zodiac sign to the next. The sign that the Moon is in at the beginning of the day (midnight Eastern Standard Time) is noted next to the quarter listing. If the Moon changes signs that day, there will be a notation saying "☽ enters" followed by the symbol for the sign it is entering.

MOON VOID-OF-COURSE: Just before the Moon enters a new sign it will make one final aspect (angular relationship) to another planet. Between that last aspect and the entrance of the Moon into the next sign it is said to be void-of-course. Activities begun when the Moon is void rarely come to fruition, or they turn out very differently than planned.

PLANETARY MOVEMENT: When a planet or asteroid moves from one sign into another, this change (called an *ingress*) is noted on the calendar pages with the exact time. The Moon and Sun are considered planets in this case. The planets (except for the Sun and Moon) can also appear to move backward as seen from the Earth. This is called a *planetary retrograde*, and is noted on the calendar pages with the symbol ℞. When the planet begins to move forward, or direct, again, it is marked D, and the time is also noted.

PLANTING AND HARVESTING DAYS: The best days for planting and harvesting are noted on the calendar pages with a seedling icon (planting) and a basket icon (harvesting).

TIME ZONE CHANGES: The times and dates of all astrological phenomena in this datebook are based on Eastern time. If you live outside of the Eastern time zone, you will need to make the following changes: Pacific Time subtract three hours; Mountain Time subtract two hours; Central Time subtract one hour; and Alaska/Hawaii subtract five hours. All data is adjusted for Daylight Saving Time.

Planets

☉	Sun	♆	Neptune
☽	Moon	♇	Pluto
☿	Mercury	⚷	Chiron
♀	Venus	⚳	Ceres
♂	Mars	⚴	Pallas
♃	Jupiter	⚵	Juno
♄	Saturn	⚶	Vesta
♅	Uranus		

Signs

♈	Aries	♐	Sagittarius
♉	Taurus	♑	Capricorn
♊	Gemini	♒	Aquarius
♋	Cancer	♓	Pisces
♌	Leo		
♍	Virgo		**Motion**
♎	Libra	℞	Retrograde
♏	Scorpio	D	Direct

1st Quarter/New Moon ☽   3rd Quarter/Full Moon: ☺
2nd Quarter ☽   4th Quarter ☽

☽ **Tuesday** ←	Day and date
1st Libra ←	Moon's quarter and sign
2nd Quarter 4:01 am ←	Moon quarter change
☽ v/c 4:01 am ←	Moon void-of-course
☽ enters ♏ 9:30 am ←	Moon sign change/ingress
♄ ℞ 10:14 am ←	Planetary retrograde
Color: Gray ←	Color of the day

Planting day → 🌱

Harvesting day → 🧺

5

Autumn Enchantment
by Ellen Dugan

Nature always wears the colors of the spirit.
—Ralph Waldo Emerson

There is something extra-enchanting about the autumn months. Perhaps it is the snap in the air or the luminous colors of the fall foliage. Apples are ripe, tart, and juicy—and just waiting to be made into pies. There are the bright jewel-tone colors of chrysanthemums and the whimsy of scarecrows guarding a home. We have bright orange pumpkins dotting the neighborhoods and rustling bundles of cornstalks standing like sentries around porch posts and entrances.

Adding a little autumn enchantment to your home and into your life is easy enough, especially when you approach it from a natural-magic perspective. So let's take a look at harvest and Halloween/Samhain decorations and add a touch of witchery to these down-to-earth items.

Apples

Apples are among the most magical of fruits. According to many mythologies it is the food that grants eternal youth and immortality to the gods. Any mortal lucky enough to get ahold of a sacred apple and consume it would then gain access to the underworld and receive the gift of prophecy.

When sliced crosswise, the apple reveals a star-shaped arrangement of seeds inside. This is sometimes referred to as the Star of Knowledge.

The apple is a "secret" symbol for the craft, and the traditional harvest game of bobbing for apples may have some ties to old divination magic. The point of this challenge or game is to test the petitioner: as the apple floats and bobs along the surface of the water, each person has to hold her breath, dunk her head in, and try to grab the apple only using her teeth (sort of an ordeal by water!). Going through water to get the apple is symbolic of the journey to Avalon (the land of apples). If the petitioner is successful, he gets to eat his apple, perhaps acquiring the ability of foresight and magic. Try it yourself this autumn: fill up an old washtub with water and float a dozen apples in it. Let your family or circle take turns, and prepare to have fun!

Autumn Leaves

Here is a great idea that won't cost you a dime: gather fall leaves and display them in an old jar or basket, or arrange them across a shelf or mantle with seasonal gourds and mini-pumpkins. You could also use these leaves as accessories in your magic. Try scarlet-brown oak leaves to invoke the wisdom of the Green Man. Use red or yellow maple leaves in charm bags to promote love or sweeten up your life. Add the luminous red leaves of the dogwood to spells and charms designed to bring love and security or to encourage a happy and protected home. Work with the soft yellow elm leaf for fairy magic and glamours (one of the folk names for the elm tree is elven). Or simply use the various colors of the leaves as part of your color magic, just like you would a candle. Match up the color of the leaf to your magical intention.

Corn Stalks and Ornamental Corn

Porch posts wrapped in golden-brown cornstalks stylishly celebrate the harvest festivals and encourage prosperity and good luck. Corn is sacred to many an earth mother goddess, so think about that the next time you go to tie a bundle of the rustling stalks to your porch. Cornstalks displayed inside, or, nowadays, outside of the home are thought to encourage fertility and to bring good luck. Plus, it really sets the stage for a lavish harvest celebration.

Ornamental corn is a popular decorative accessory for the fall months. Sometimes referred to as "Indian corn," these brightly colored ears come in a rainbow of jewel-tones and colors. Try stringing up ears of ornamental corn into garlands that can be tied to the porch, hung above doorways, or laid across the mantle.

If creating swags and garlands with ornamental corn just isn't your thing, then consider something a bit less complicated. Typically, ornamental corn is sold in bunches of three, which you could use to symbolize the three harvest festivals of Lammas, Mabon, and Samhain, or to represent the Maiden, Mother, and Crone. Hang a trio of corn on your front door or living room wall and enchant them for fertility, prosperity, and protection. Try out this autumn enchantment as you fasten the ears of corn up for display:

> *This golden season of autumn I now celebrate;*
> *Blessed be the harvest, make strong my magical faith.*
> *Three ears of corn for the Maiden, the Mother, and the Crone;*
> *Lady bless this house with abundance, and make it your own.*

Chrysanthemums

In flower magic the chrysanthemum invokes protection. This time of year, when the veil between our world and the world of spirit is at its thinnest, mums come in pretty handy. Sure, we all know that Halloween/Samhain is famous for its free-roaming spooks, but how about using a little flower magic to ensure that only the good-natured ones find their way to your door on October 31? These fabulous and inexpensive flowers are available in many colors and varieties, which makes choosing the right mum for color magic a snap! Try red mums for love and yellow mums to encourage joy and good cheer. Purple mums bring power and passion, white mums invoke the truth, and bronze tones encourage a loving and happy home. Try setting out a few pots of mysterious mums with your pumpkins this autumn to protect your property and your pets, and to encourage love, happiness, power, and protection for your family. Here is a fall flower charm to go along with your mum magic:

> *The chrysanthemum is a magical flower indeed,*
> *It brings love, joy, and protection with all possible speed.*
> *In this season of autumn, I spin this fall flower spell,*
> *Believe in this natural magic and all will be well.*

Pumpkins

What is Halloween or Samhain without a pumpkin? It's hard to imagine this holiday without the glowing and flickering faces of jack-o'-lanterns lining the streets or perched on top of porches, stumps, and hay bales. This native squash became popular as a replacement vegetable for the Irish custom of using turnips or hollowed-out cabbages. Pumpkins can be grown just

about anywhere—including six out of the seven continents! The original purpose for jack-o'-lanterns was to frighten away evil spirits, so consider using your Halloween/Samhain pumpkins in conjunction with a little candle magic to frighten away negativity and bad luck this year.

I recommend black, patchouli-scented votives in holders. These are readily available in the fall months at most arts-and-crafts or department stores. Patchouli is a protective scent, and its musky, spicy aroma smells wonderful. If you can find some, stock up. Carve a hideous face on your pumpkin, or any witchy design that you prefer—or try those pumpkin-carving kits, which are fun, easy, and have lots of magical designs. Once your jack-o'-lantern is carved and ready to go, place the candle holder inside and drop in the scented votive. As you light the candle, repeat the following charm three times:

Bright pumpkins that glow, and scented candles of black,
Send bad luck away, turn negativity back.
By all the enchantment of three times three,
Lady hear my spell on this Hallowed Eve.

Why not cast a witchy eye on all of the beautiful, natural bounty that nature has to offer us at this time of year and see what sort of autumn enchantment you can conjure up? Take a fresh look at nature and see what sort of new, elemental spin you can put on your own individualized magic. Have a blessed autumn, a bountiful harvest, a soulful Samhain, and, of course, a happy Halloween!

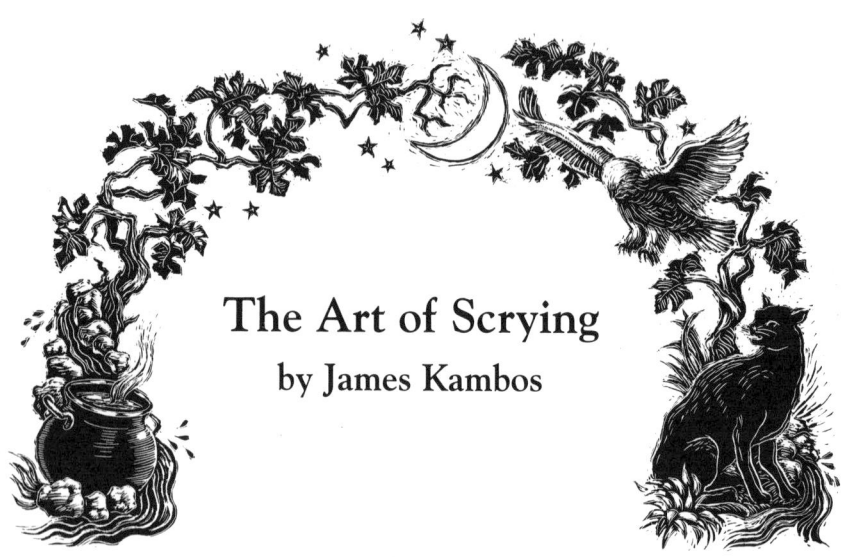

The Art of Scrying
by James Kambos

Not far from my boyhood home there was a secluded pond known as Avon Pond. Located in a forest clearing, just off a dead-end road and surrounded by towering pine trees, the pond was the perfect secret meeting place for country kids. Sitting at the water's edge, my friends and I would fish or spin wild tales. Sometimes we'd shatter the mirror-smooth surface by skimming stones across the water.

Occasionally, I'd go to the pond alone and enjoy the solitude, gazing into the water and daydreaming. After awhile, I'd notice my own reflection would begin to fade, and in its place I'd see other images. Sometimes another face would appear, or perhaps I'd see the outline of a building. At other times I'd see shapes that couldn't be explained. I could do this until my attention was interrupted—maybe by the call of a bird, or the gentle rippling of the water as a fish swam near the surface.

At the time, although I didn't realize it, I was unconsciously scrying. Simply defined, scrying is the ancient magical art of seeing past, present, or future events and situations by gazing at a reflective surface.

The Origins of Scrying

Like many magical practices, scrying is as old as the human race. We may never know for certain what scrying method was first used, but one of the most common theories is that a body of water, such as a pond or lake, was the first scrying surface. This is quite possible, especially if the light of a Full Moon was reflected on the water's surface.

The popular image of some-one gazing at a crystal ball while scrying probably didn't occur until later in our history. Before crystal or glass balls appeared, highly polished dark-colored stones such as obsidian or jet may have been used. Any stone used for this purpose was highly prized and carefully guarded, since it absorbed the power of its user. Such stones were passed from one generation to the

next and became cherished heirlooms. Dr. John Dee, the famous British occultist who served the royal court of Queen Elizabeth I, owned such a stone. In historical documents it was referred to as a "magic mirror," but it was actually a slab of polished stone. Some sources say it was coal, though others say it was jet, or the volcanic glass obsidian.

Mirrors have also been associated with scrying for centuries. Witches of Thessaly in ancient Greece were believed to divine by using mirrors. And naturally when we think of magic mirrors we will always be reminded of the sorceress in the fairy tale *Snow White*, asking the age-old question, "Mirror, mirror on the wall, who is the fairest of them all?"

One of the most fascinating pieces of folklore concerning scrying comes to us from the Middle East. Occultists in this region believe it was the magical jinn (genies), who taught humans about the mystical art we now call scrying. The history of scrying will always be veiled with mystery, however, like the Unseen Realm itself. The origins of this form of divination may never be known, but we do know it is rooted deep in antiquity.

Scrying Tools

Any surface or object used for scrying is called a *speculum*. There is a wide range of specula available for use in scrying; many are very inexpensive and easy to find. Interestingly enough, most of the scrying tools used by today's modern Witch were also used by the magicians of long ago. When selecting a scrying tool, use your imagination. Let your instincts be your guide; you must have an affinity for whatever you choose and become intimate with it. To prevent your speculum from absorbing any unwanted energy, let no one else handle it.

What follows is a list describing items that could be used for scrying. This is only an introductory guide and is by no means exhaustive. Select a speculum that "speaks" to you.

Lakes and Ponds

Long before mirrors or glass were used for scrying, the calm waters found in lakes and ponds aided early magicians seeking visions. Just as I found as a child, gazing at water can trigger psychic abilities. If possible, gazing at water under the light of a Full Moon is best. If you scry with water, thank the water spirits by leaving a token of thanks: flower petals or a special herb, sprinkled upon the water, would be appropriate. If you choose water-gazing as your scrying method, it's a good idea to use the same location each time. That way you'll create a place of power that only you know about.

Bowls and Bottles

During the days when Witches were persecuted, possessing any object related to magic was dangerous. Witches then began to use items that could be found in any home to do their magical work—for example, bowls or colored bottles. Since these were ordinary household items, they could be left out in the open without arousing suspicion.

To use a bowl for scrying, select a dark-colored bowl and fill it with water. A dark-colored bottle is also good, but needn't be filled with liquid to be used as a speculum. Cauldrons also make a good choice for scrying, since they're similar in shape to a bowl. Fill one with water and, if you wish, drop a silver coin into the bottom: this will serve as a focal point to help increase psychic abilities as you gaze.

Olive Oil

The use of this sacred oil as a scrying medium is ancient, but not well known outside the Mediterranean region. Place about a tablespoon of olive oil in a bowl of water. When the droplets of oil form a circle, you may begin to scry, gazing into the oil as it floats on the water. This scrying method was used by the wise women of the Mediterranean to discover who cast the dreaded evil eye.

Mirrors

As I stated earlier, divining with mirrors is an ancient art dating back to the Persians. The ancient Greeks and Romans also scryed with mirrors. Since mirrors have such a smooth, shiny surface, they easily serve as a portal to the spiritual realm. Round or oval mirrors are best, since they echo the shapes of the Moon and the egg—both potent magical symbols.

If you're able to make a mirror yourself, that adds extra power to it, but I've seen beautifully crafted mirrors at occult shops and in catalogs that would serve the purpose equally well. Old mirrors found in antique shops are also special; however, they should be ritually cleansed during a waxing Moon before use. If you do make your own magic mirror, begin during a New Moon to connect with the power of the waxing Moon. When not in use, your mirror should be kept covered and out of sight; never use it for any other purpose.

An alternative to a mirror is the old curved glass found in antique picture frames. To use these old glass pieces as a speculum, first cleanse and bless the glass during a waxing Moon. Next, apply about three coats of black acrylic paint to the concave or back side of the glass, and let it dry. Frame and embellish your "gazing glass" as you wish. Bless and consecrate according to your beliefs, then use. Like the mirror, your glass should be kept covered with a dark cloth and hidden when not in use.

Crystal and Glass Spheres

Spheres made of quartz or glass, known commonly as crystal balls, are among the best known scrying tools. Authentic crystal balls are expensive and probably weren't used by the village wise ones of long ago; it's my guess that actual crystal balls were originally used by ceremonial magicians. Crystal does have the advantage of drawing you into its energy field as you work with it, but glass spheres are less expensive and make fine substitutes for crystal. To tell the difference between a glass and crystal ball, remember that genuine crystal will always be cool to the touch, and may contain interior veins or other marks. Protect your sphere by wrapping it in a black silk or cotton cloth. Keep it away from sunlight, but occasionally expose it to the light of a Full Moon.

How to Scry

You don't need superhuman psychic powers to master scrying techniques. It just takes a quiet, relaxed atmosphere and plenty of practice.

Place your speculum before you on a flat surface. Darken the room. Place a lighted candle behind you, but don't let the flame be reflected

directly by your scrying surface. Light incense if you wish. Center, and gaze into the speculum. Blink naturally. Concentrate on a single question. The scrying surface will begin to mist over, then it will become clear. Now expect an image to appear. The image may be as clear as a photo, or it might be nothing but symbols. You may see movement as if you were watching a movie. Some individuals see colors, others black and white. Just let the images flow. Gradually the visions will fade.

Keep your gazing sessions short: about ten to fifteen minutes. Let yourself return to reality slowly, as you'll probably be in a light meditative state. Give thanks and put away your tools. If nothing happens, try again in a few days. Scrying can't be rushed or performed on demand.

As you become more confident with your scrying abilities, you'll gain unlimited magical potential. You'll be able to gain insight into past, present, and future events. You may choose to contact a guardian spirit or uncover past lives. The magical possibilities are endless.

Further Reading

Buckland, Raymond. *Secrets of Gypsy Fortunetelling*. St. Paul: Llewellyn, 1988.

Cunningham, Scott. *Earth Power*. St. Paul: Llewellyn, 1983.

Tyson, Donald. *How To Make and Use a Magic Mirror*. St. Paul: Llewellyn, 1990.

Stone Magic
by Gerina Dunwich

Stones, like all natural objects, are said to contain inherent mystical energy vibrations that can be used for healing, spellcasting, and divination. Many contemporary practitioners of magic (from folk traditions to ceremonial) are drawn to stones; however, the use of stones as a tool of the occult arts dates back to ancient (and probably prehistoric) times.

Stones are used in magical workings for numerous purposes and in a variety of ways. They are most commonly employed for healing, protection against the evil eye, attracting love and good luck, balancing the chakras, and warding off bad luck and hexes. Many magical practitioners also use them for invoking deities, conjuring spirits, summoning and banishing demons, controlling the weather, and divining the future.

Stones are worn as talismanic rings or pendants, carried in charm bags, placed on altars, and even powdered and added to potions, candles, and incense mixtures. They can also be used to outline magic circles, make healing tonics, and add power to ritual tools. Some people even attach them to the collars of their pets and familiars to keep them safe from harm.

Stone magic is generally uncomplicated, yet can yield powerful results for those who know the magical properties of precious and semi-precious stones. But before using any stone as a tool to help manifest your intentions, it is important that it be ritually cleansed (or cleared) and then charged. Cleansing removes negative vibrations from a stone without affecting its magical properties, while charging programs it with energy.

Cleansing

There are numerous methods for cleansing stones and crystals, but the most popular ones include soaking them in saltwater or sea water for a minimum of twenty-four hours, holding them (with their termination pointing downward) under cold-running tap water for at least one minute, placing them in direct sunlight from mid-morning until mid-afternoon, burying them in the ground for at least seven days, covering them with sea salt for one to seven days, visualizing them surrounded by a white or golden light beaming from your third eye chakra, stroking them with a tape de-magnetizer, soaking them in sage tea, exhaling upon them, smudging them with incense or dried herbs, and petitioning a deity to purify and bless them.

Whatever cleansing method you use is entirely a matter of personal choice, and can be based on magical tradition, spiritual beliefs, or perceptions of energy. If you are unsure which method is best for your stone, allow your own intuition to be your guide or consult an oracle such as a pendulum.

The amount of time required for cleansing depends on the amount of negative energy that needs to be cleared. A small amount of negativity may take a few minutes to a few hours to clear, while a large amount may require several days to a week or longer.

A stone that has absorbed a great deal of negativity over a period of time will give off negative vibrations, which can be felt by psychic-sensitive persons as either a subtle or intense negative energy current. Aura readers will sometimes perceive it as a dark mist or halo emanating from the crystal or stone.

If you do healing work with crystals and stones, or have them on

display in your home, and find yourself frequently experiencing headaches, depression, feelings of inertia, and/or unexplained physical illnesses, this may be a warning sign that they are giving off negative vibrations and need to be cleansed.

After your stone has been ritually cleansed, hold it in your receptive hand (the left if you're right-handed, and the right if you're left-handed). If its energy vibrations feel normal to you, this indicates a successful cleansing. (The more you work with stones, the more familiar you will become with their different energies.) But if you perceive the energy as unhealthy, disturbing in any way, or just "not right," then the cleansing process will need to be repeated until that feeling goes away.

When acquiring a new stone, always perform a ritual cleansing to remove any past influences from it. Stones used for healing work should be thoroughly cleansed before each and every use and after being handled by people other than the healer.

Stones that have been used for negative purposes (such as hexing or the conjuring of evil entities) should never be employed for any type of positive spell work (especially healings) unless they are thoroughly cleansed beforehand.

Charging

Charging a stone is relatively simple and can be accomplished in the following manner. On the first night of the Full Moon (when lunar energies are at their peak) place the stone in your power hand (this is the hand with which you normally use to write). As you hold it, visualize your specific need or desire, and will your energy to flow from your hand into the stone. Continue doing this until you feel that the stone is attuned to your energies and vibrating with your personal power. Repeat the charging process prior to each spell or ritual you perform.

Intentions

The following is a list of various magical intentions, followed by the stones most commonly associated with them:

Animals

Boulder matrix opal (to access one's animal guides), cat's-eye (for spellwork relating to cats), cylindrite, faustite, ganophyllite, horne-blende (for communicating with the physical and spiritual animal worlds), stibnite (a totem stone for the wolf), and tiger's-eye.

Bravery

Agate (tawny), amethyst, aquamarine, beryl, bloodstone, carnelian, diamond, garnet, lapis lazuli, sard, sardonyx, tiger's-eye, tourmaline (red), and turquoise.

Divination

Azurite, emerald, flint, hematite, jet, lamprophyllite, mica, moonstone, mosandrite, obsidian, opal, palermoite (stimulates the ability for palmistry), sapphire, and tiger's-eye.

Dreams

Amethyst, augelite, azurite, beta quartz, Chinese writing rock, dickite, garnet, jade, jasper (red), kyanite, lapis lazuli, manganosite, moonstone, opal, peridot, quartz crystal, rhonite, ruby, sapphire (green), and tourmaline (blue).

Fairy Magic

Cross stone (a form of andalusite), flint (also known as elf-arrow, elf-shot, and fairy-shot, and once used by the Irish to ward off mischievous fairy-folk), holey stones (to see fairies), and staurolite (also known as fairy-cross, fairy-stone, and fairy-tears).

Good Luck

Alexandrite, amber, Apache tear, aventurine, chalcedony, chrysoprase, cross stone, jade, jet, lepidolite, moonstone, olivine, opal (black), pearl, ruby, sardonyx, tiger's-eye, topaz, and turquoise.

Grounding

Calcite (pink), hematite, jasper (brown), kunzite, moonstone, obsidian, petalite, smoky quartz, tourmaline (black), zircon (brown, also known as malacon).

Love Magic

Agate, alexandrite, amber, amethyst, beryl, calcite, chrysocolla, emerald, jade, lapis lazuli, lepidolite, lodestone, magnetite, malachite, moonstone, olivine, pearl, rhodocrosite, rose quartz, sapphire, sard, topaz, tourmaline (pink), and turquoise.

Magical Power (to increase)

Amber, bloodstone, calcite, magnetite, malachite, opal, quartz crystal, and ruby.

Magical Self-Defense

Bloodstone, garnet, jade, jasper (red), lava rock, onyx, pipestone, rhodocrosite, rhodonite, ruby, sardonyx, sapphire, and tourmaline (red).

Money, Prosperity, Wealth

Aventurine, bloodstone, calcite, cat's eye, chrysoprase, emerald, jade, mother-of-pearl, olivine, opal, pearl, peridot, ruby, sapphire, spinel, staurolite, tiger's-eye, topaz, tourmaline (green), and zircon.

Nightmares (to prevent)

Chalcedony, citrine, coral, garnet, jet, lepidolite, and ruby.

Protection

Agate, amber, Apache tear, beryl, calcite, carnelian, cat's-eye (especially against the evil eye), chalcedony, chrysoprase, citrine, coral, diamond, emerald, garnet, jade, jasper, jet, lapis lazuli, lepidolite, magnetite, malachite, marble, mica, moonstone, mother-of-pearl, obsidian, olivine, onyx (against the evil eye), pearl, peridot, pumice, quartz crystal, ruby, sapphire (against the evil eye), sard, sardonyx, serpentine, staurolite, sunstone, tiger's-eye, topaz, tourmaline (black), tourmaline (red), turquoise, zircon (clear), and zircon (red).

Psychic Powers (to awaken or strengthen)

Agate (rose-eye), amethyst, apatite, aquamarine, azurite, beryl, bloodstone, cherry opal, citrine, emerald, jet, lapis lazuli, lavender quartz, lepidolite, mica, moonstone, obsidian (purple), opal, petalite, quartz crystal, sapphire, smithsonite, and sugilite.

Strength (physical)

Agate, amber, beryl, bloodstone, diamond, garnet, jasper (red), onyx, pipestone, ruby, sard, sardonyx, and tourmaline (red).

Wisdom

Agate, aventurine, chrysocolla, coral, jade, jasper (mottled), mica, pumice, sapphire, sodalite, and sugilite.

Cause and Effect
by Julianna Yau

Witches turn to many sources to deepen their spiritual connection to and intellectual understanding of their practices—for example, other religions, holistic health, and mythology. But many other sources are available to enrich a Witch's knowledge—and one of the sources that is often overlooked is philosophy. Philosophy can be very useful to Witches, because philosophers explore vast and often abstract concepts. Among the topics explored by philosophers is the notion of causality.

One of the standard teachings of magical work is that one should not try to direct the exact route of the energy released by a spell. This is a strongly held practice because such an attempt would either limit the course of the energy to the directed goal or cause undesirable results that were unforeseen by the practitioner. However, it doesn't imply that practitioners of magic shouldn't have a deeper understanding of causality.

A knowledge of causality is important to Witches: the concept of magic, whether in the form of spells or rituals, is based heavily in concepts of causality. Many texts on witchcraft give a straightforward and simple explanation of causality: decide what you want, focus your energy toward your goal, release the energy, and let nature run her course. But since causality is so vital to the magical process, why not take a deeper look at it?

If you have encountered any basic philosophical teachings, you have probably heard of a philosopher named David Hume. One of his more well-known ideas was that people don't have any reasonable proof that cause and effect exist. He argued that because we can't actually see the effect of one event on another, we can't claim that one thing caused an effect on something else. Hume basically argued that causality is simply something conjured in our minds, rather than something that exists in reality.

This reasoning frustrates not only Witches, but many philosophers also. One such philosopher is Immanuel Kant, who argued that an event is the natural result of a cause, and doesn't have to be tied to that cause by something visible. His position is that laws of causality must exist to regulate the events of nature.

So what does all of this philosophical rambling have to do with the practice of magic?

Unlike Hume's philosophy, witchcraft's philosophy teaches that one does not need to see effect to know that it exists. Causality is understood as something that must and does occur. Also, causality exists not only for magic but also for everyday existence. It works on many levels, from physical laws that affect everything that exists to economic and social laws that only work in certain areas for certain people.

In mundane life, people rely on the consistency of their actions' results to determine what they can do in the future to obtain the results they desire. Likewise, Witches compare the results of one magical act with those of a similar magical act to determine if there is any consistency. Practiced Witches urge newly initiated Witches to record such comparisons (and the original act of magic) in a Book of Shadows. Experienced Witches know that a collection of detailed records that show what has been done, and what the results were, will help one decide what action needs to be done to make something happen through magic.

Essentially, this practice is meant to help Witches understand the way cause and effect operate in the magical realm. Without such an understanding, magic would seem to be without defense— merely a collection of superstitious actions. For many Witches, a magical act is one based upon the experience of former magical acts. The spells that are passed on to new Witches are ones that have been

proven to work by practiced Witches. New spells are formed with the knowledge of what has worked in the past. Witches use this information to create a spell for a circumstance that has not previously occurred.

Witches must always be careful to be able to identify which aspects of their magical acts could have caused the results that followed. Was it a specific action, or was it a special combination of actions? What aspect of the timing and spatial placement could have caused the results? These are questions that Witches have been taught to ask themselves because the answers can help them understand the key to creating similar results from a magical act in the future.

By using the records from a Book of Shadows, a Witch can also determine what aspect of a magical act has not affected the outcome of that act. This is useful because a Witch who wishes to perform a concise magical act (because an elaborate one is not possible or desirable) is then able to perform only the actions that are absolutely necessary.

Aside from magic itself, causality is also important to Witches because of their adherence to the Law of Three. Also known as the Rule of Three or the Rule/Law of Threefold Return, this concept states that any action performed is returned threefold to the performer. This concept is applied not only to magical acts but also to actions performed in everyday life. Their adherence to the Law of Three makes most Witches very aware of causality.

On an ethical level, awareness of the Law of Three encourages people to do good rather than evil. With regards to the concerns of causality, awareness of the Law of Three makes awareness of causality a constant concern. One must be aware that anything one does may cause oneself to be on the receiving end of a similar action. The Law of Three promotes a basic understanding of causality because it makes use of a more direct effect.

Magical acts and the Law of Three use causality in different ways. With magic, one performs ritualistic actions that cause a result which is not directly related to the action itself. A Witch may light a candle with the intent of amplifying his or her chances of success; although the intent is clear and directed, the lighting of a candle is not actually the equivalent of success. If a Witch were to increase the chances of success by using the Law of Three, he or she would perform actions that are directly related to success, whether they are for the benefit of themselves or others.

Causality is an integral part of a Witch's consciousness, regardless of how aware that Witch is of the actual concepts. Causality is "in effect" for all of a Witch's life, whether it be in his or her everyday actions through the Law of Three or in magical acts. Although David Hume may argue that we can't prove causality exists, he did say that it is best for us to assume that it does exist—because otherwise our understanding of the world would fall apart. Maybe a scientific proof of the existence of cause and effect was unsatisfactory for him, but for everyone who believes in magic, cause and effect are undeniably present in every aspect of life.

Further Reading

Hume, David. *An Enquiry Concerning Human Understanding.* Oxford Philosophical Texts. London: Oxford Press, 1999.

Hume, David. *A Treatise of Human Nature.* Oxford Philosophical Texts. London: Oxford Press, 2000.

Kant, Immanuel. *Practical Philosophy.* New York: Cambridge University Press, 1999.

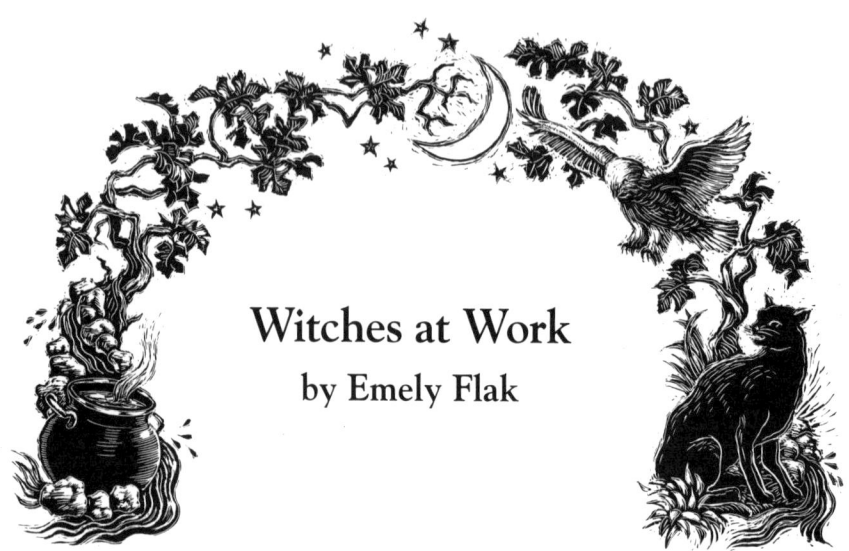

Witches at Work
by Emely Flak

Do you spend most of your waking hours in a competitive work environment? Do you ever wonder if your Wiccan ethics are compatible with this often dog-eat-dog work jungle? People like we Pagans may ask: How can I live by my spiritual values and make a difference at work? How do I reconcile my spiritual choice in a cutthroat corporate world? These are some of the challenges facing the modern, urban Witch.

The traditional company or employer tends to focus on tools and strategies that people use in the workplace to carry out their jobs. The good news is that contemporary organizations now focus on their human assets and ways to optimize their employees' potential. For a long time, we were led to believe that our professional and private lives were two separate entities. The clever companies have recognized that spirituality and harmony are part of their employees' lives, and cannot be separated from the workplace.

We are starting to hear about companies that provide meditation rooms and quiet gardens to promote a work/life balance. They sponsor activities like lunchtime or after-work yoga classes to keep their staff members happy. These progressive employers have realized that with the disproportionate amount of time many of us spend at work, it's difficult to separate our professional lives from our spiritual lives—and that employees are likely to be more productive in a happier environment. This shift has given rise to terms like "organizations with soul" and "spirit at work." An organization with "soul" promotes spiritual values such as respect, teamwork, and harmony in the workplace. In the new economy, words like "spirituality" appear more frequently in management dialogue. In this corporate climate, you can apply Pagan principles to positively affect your workplace. You can be a corporate Witch and maintain a sense of balance.

Values

Despite these trends, there is a perception that it can be difficult to find a job where the organizational values are aligned with your own personal values. When looking at a potential workplace, ask yourself: To what extent does the culture of the organization match what I value? If there is little or no alignment, then you will find it difficult to match its values with your personal ethics. In fact, some corporate activities will probably never agree with your values.

However, you can try to find a way to close that gap. For example, a woman I knew worked for a company that sold gambling services and products. Because she believed that it was unethical to make a large profit from a person's gambling weakness, it seemed that the organization's values failed to match her own. The gap was closed when she found out that her employer had formed a Responsible Gambling Committee in response to community concern. Her employer welcomed her interest in the group. As part of her job, she now actively contributes to ethical gaming issues. This helped her reconcile her personal values with those of her employer, and she performs her work with a renewed sense of purpose.

Speak or Remain Silent?

You may be wondering, "Can I practice my Wiccan values at work without telling everyone that I am a Witch?" Before you scream your Pagan pride at work, ask yourself: What is my position on the organizational chart? How many runs do I have on the board as a professional? How conservative are the senior managers and executives? What do I have to gain from disclosure? What is the potential impact from coming out as a Witch? Could it be career-limiting or career-enhancing for me?

This is a risk analysis only you can make, depending on these factors. The impact your Pagan friend made in another company when coming out is not a reliable indicator of the reaction you will receive. Every place is different. Equal opportunity legislation is not an infallible protection of human diversity.

In my day job (in corporate land) I certainly wear my pentacle ring, but will only talk about the Wiccan path if I am asked. If in any doubt, it's advisable to keep your witchy ways under your pointed hat.

Making a Difference?

Whether or not you have announced your Wiccan ways, you can help make your work environment a better place for you and your colleagues.

For example, follow the Wiccan Rede in the workplace: never act against the free will of another. Resist the temptation to work magic that interferes with another person, regardless of how badly that colleague or boss has behaved. Instead, focus on your protection. Also, you can lead by example. By remembering the law of karma, set an example of positive and ethical behavior to your team, your managers, and your subordinates. Above all, be positive. Give positive feedback to colleagues, managers, and subordinates when it's deserved. Very few managers recognize the motivating power of patting someone on the back. Spread positive energy and it will be returned to you.

Your Sacred Space

If your employer is not "enlightened," you can still create your sacred space in your work area to nourish your spiritual essence. Although it is unlikely you can set up a full altar on or near your desk, there are some things you can do to affirm that connection with your spirit.

For instance, have items that remind you of nature. This can be a photograph, a shell, or a rock. Play music, if you can. Your favorite sounds will uplift you, even if you can only listen on headphones. You can also surround your work area with inspirational quotations and change them regularly.

Sacred space is not intended to be a promotion of your path to others. It provides visual and auditory messages that are unique to you, to provide you with a source of focus and inspiration.

Life Balance

Despite good employer intentions, and the fact that you can express yourself spiritually at work, it's very easy to neglect yourself with a hectic lifestyle. One simple way to nurture yourself is to develop a ritual that clearly declares your sacred space at home. The Japanese custom of leaving shoes outside the home to symbolize leaving worries at the door is one way of achieving this. One Wiccan friend told me that her first activity when she arrives home is to take a ritual shower. In the shower, she visualizes any negative work-

place energy washing away and down the drain. Make your home a sanctuary where you can truly relax and recharge.

The gap between personal and professional ethics is often a perceived one, and it can be closed. With some careful application you can be both a corporate warrior and a Witch. You don't need to come out of the broom closet to integrate your Wiccan values in your workplace. The workplace may not always be fun, but it can be an expression of who you are. The roles you perform at work make up a significant part of your learning journey, so make the most of it. Even if your employer is not an organization with soul, take your spirit to work and make a positive difference!

Further Reading

Cunningham, Scott. *Wicca: A Guide for the Solitary Practitioner.* St. Paul: Llewellyn, 1990.

Trobe, Kala. *The Witch's Guide to Life.* St. Paul: Llewellyn, 2003.

27 Monday
3rd ♋
Color: Lavender

28 Tuesday
3rd ♋
☽ v/c 2:34 am
☽ enters ♌ 12:14 pm
Color: White

Moonstone is a safe-travelers stone; keep a small
tumbled moonstone in your pocket while you travel

29 Wednesday
3rd ♌
Color: Topaz

30 Thursday
3rd ♌
☽ v/c 9:54 am
Color: Green

31 Friday
3rd ♌
☽ enters ♍ 12:33 am
Color: Purple

Light a fresh white candle at midnight on New Year's Eve;
say a prayer for prosperity and health for the new year

Set in Eastern Standard Time (EST)

January

The common era calendar shows us that 2005 will begin with a waning crescent Moon in Libra. If we accept that what happens when the year changes affects the year to come, we not only have to recognize that Libra is a sign of balance, peace, attractiveness, and friendship, but also that those attributes are on the wane.

As the year changes from 2004 to 2005, allow yourself to go into a meditative state. Concentrate on how much the world needs Libran attributes, how your state and city need them, and how you and your own family or coven need them.

As you sit in contemplation, close your eyes to avoid distractions and use a simple chant to keep your mind focused.

> *Through Libra goes the waning Moon,*
> *And to her traits and energy we attune.*
> *Mother Moon wrinkles, receives her crone powers,*
> *We cull Libra's traits to balance ours.*

—Edain McCoy

---

1 Saturday
3rd ♍
Color: Black

Kwanzaa ends
New Year's Day
Birthday of Sir James Frazer,
author of *The Golden Bough*, 1854

---

2 Sunday
3rd ♍
☽ v/c 1:23 am
☽ enters ♎ 11:19 am
Color: Yellow

January

◑ Monday

3rd ♎
4th Quarter 12:46 pm
Color: Gray

Death of Edgar Cayce, psychic, 1945

4 Tuesday

4th ♎
☽ v/c 9:20 am
☽ enters ♏ 7:00 pm
Color: Red

Aquarian Tabernacle Church
registered in Australia by
Lady Tamara Von Forslun, 1994

5 Wednesday

4th ♏
Color: Brown

6 Thursday

4th ♏
☽ v/c 1:29 pm
☽ enters ♐ 10:44 pm
Color: Green

Twelfth Night/Epiphany
Patricia Crowther's witchcraft
radio show, A *Spell of Witchcraft*,
airs in Britain, 1971

7 Friday

4th ♐
Color: White

8 Saturday

4th ♐
☽ v/c 10:02 pm
☽ enters ♑ 11:11 pm
Color: Indigo

Birthday of MacGregor Mathers,
one of the three original founders
of the Golden Dawn, 1854
Death of Dion Fortune, 1946

9 Sunday

4th ♑
♀ enters ♑ 11:56 am
☿ enters ♑ 11:09 pm
Color: Orange

Jamie Dodge wins lawsuit against
the Salvation Army, which fired her
based on her Wiccan religion, 1989

January

☽ Monday

4th ♑
New Moon 7:03 am
☽ v/c 12:58 pm
☽ enters ♒ 10:07 pm
Color: Lavender

Oil of vanilla conveys self-confidence and brings good fortune

11 Tuesday
1st ♒
♅ enters ♈ 4:36 am
Color: Black

12 Wednesday
1st ♒
☽ v/c 10:44 am
☽ enters ♓ 9:50 pm
Color: White

Mary Smith hanged in England; she had quarreled with neighbors, who said that the Devil appeared to her as a black man, 1616

13 Thursday
1st ♓
Color: Turquoise

Final witchcraft laws repealed in Austria, 1787

14 Friday
1st ♓
☽ v/c 3:22 pm
Color: Pink

Official Confession of Error by jurors of Salem Witch trials, 1696

Human Be-In, a Pagan-style festival, takes place in San Francisco, attended by Timothy Leary and Allen Ginsburg, 1967

Set in Eastern Standard Time (EST)

The Trail to Patience

Give to me patience, one grain at a time.
Bring me divinity; make me serene.
Lend me tranquility—sudden, sublime.
Give to me patience, one grain at a time.
Show me the mountain road worth the
*   long climb.*
Send me along to share what I've seen.
Give me to patience, one grain at a time.
Let my divinity make all serene.
                                    —Elizabeth Barrette

15 Saturday
1st ♓
☽ enters ♈ 12:27 am
Color: Gray

16 Sunday
1st ♈
Color: Gold

Birthday of Dr. Dennis Carpenter,
Circle Sanctuary

January

◐ Monday

1st ♈
2nd Quarter 1:57 am
☽ v/c 1:57 am
☽ enters ♉ 7:06 am
Color: White

Birthday of Martin Luther King, Jr. (observed)

18 Tuesday

2nd ♉
Color: Maroon

19 Wednesday

2nd ♉
☽ v/c 5:19 pm
☽ enters ♊ 5:24 pm
☉ enters ♒ 6:22 pm
Color: Yellow

Sun enters Aquarius
Birthday of Dorothy Clutterbuck,
who initiated Gerald Gardner, 1880

20 Thursday

2nd ♊
Color: Purple

Inauguration Day

21 Friday

2nd ♊
☽ v/c 4:26 pm
Color: Rose

Celtic Tree Month of Rowan begins

Set in Eastern Standard Time (EST)

Fabulous Fondue

½ lb. Gruyere
½ lb. Emmentaler
(or 1 lb. American Swiss)
¼ cup flour
1 clove of garlic
2 cups dry white wine
3 tbs. Kirsch or cognac

Grate cheese and toss with flour. Halve the clove of garlic and rub around the inside of the fondue pot, then discard. Heat wine until just starting to bubble up from the bottom. You can either do this in an electric fondue pot or, if using an earthenware fondue, heat the wine in a separate pot on the stove and then transfer it to the earthenware pot and light the burner under it. Add cheese in handfuls and stir until melted. Once all the cheese is melted, add Kirsch and stir until well blended. For dipping, I recommend French or Italian bread, cubed; pieces of cooked sausage or ham; carrot, broccoli, and celery slices. Serve with salad and a white wine.

—ShadowCat

---

22 Saturday

2nd ♊
☽ enters ♋ 5:42 am
Color: Black

Hanging round-shaped sun-catchers in the windows promotes harmony, adds rainbows, and brings positive chi to any room

---

23 Sunday

2nd ♋
Color: Amber

January

24 Monday
2nd ♋
☽ v/c 4:17 am
☽ enters ♌ 6:21 pm
Color: Silver

Wear patchouli oil when taking a test
to clear the mind and sharpen the wits

☺ Tuesday
2nd ♌
Full Moon 5:32 am
Color: Scarlet

Cold Moon
Birthday of Robert Burns, Scottish poet, 1759

26 Wednesday
3rd ♌
☽ v/c 5:39 pm
Color: Topaz

27 Thursday
3rd ♌
☽ enters ♍ 6:24 am
Color: White

28 Friday
3rd ♍
Color: Coral

Tuck a green aventurine and a bloodstone in the cash
register drawer to encourage lots of business and sales

The Persistence of Stone

I want one thing to call my own,
Embodied in the bones of Earth:
The stern persistence of a stone.
I want one thing to call my own,
Persistence out of granite grown:
A stately measure of my worth.
I want this thing to call my own,
Embodied in the bones of Earth.

—Elizabeth Barrette

29 Saturday
3rd ♍
☽ v/c 4:07 pm
☽ enters ♎ 5:13 pm
Color: Blue

30 Sunday
3rd ♎
☿ enters ♒ 12:37 am
Color: Orange

Birthday of Zsusanna Budapest,
feminist Witch

31 Monday

3rd ♎
☽ v/c 10:21 pm
Color: Ivory

Dr. Fian, believed to be the head
of the North Berwick Witches, found
guilty and executed for witchcraft in
Scotland by personal order of King
James VI (James I of England), 1591

1 Tuesday

3rd ♎
☽ enters ♏ 1:51 am
♀ ℞ 5:27 am
♃ ℞ 9:26 pm
Color: Black

The snowdrop, crocus, and African violet are traditional
flowers with which to celebrate the sabbat of Imbolc

○ Wednesday

3rd ♏
4th Quarter 2:27 am
♀ enters ♒ 10:42 am
☽ v/c 5:56 pm
Color: Brown

Imbolc
Groundhog Day
Leo Martello becomes a third-degree
Welsh traditionalist, 1973

3 Thursday

4th ♏
☽ enters ♐ 7:21 am
Color: Green

Imbolc crossquarter day
(Sun reaches 15° Aquarius)

4 Friday

4th ♐
Color: Pink

Imbolc

Finally, the days are getting longer. The darkest time of the year is over. In Celtic tradition, this is the holiday of Brigid, who rules smithcraft, poetry, and healing. She is very much a goddess of fire and transformation. Fire is necessary for smithing—the transformation of metal. Healing is a kind of transformation. The inspiration necessary for poetry is a transformation as well.

It is traditional on Imbolc, at sunset, to light candles in every window in the house to honor the goddess of light. To prepare yourself, take a ritual bath, lit by candles and scented with incense if possible. Put out all the lights and blow out the candles. Go to the easternmost door or window, light a white candle, and say, "Brigid be with us, Brigid inspire us, Brigid be with us." Go clockwise through the house, lighting the candles, reciting this chant. If you live in a two-story house, start on the top floor. After you have lit the house, return to the place you started, and, chant, "Brigid is with us, Brigid is with us, Brigid is with us." You can put out most of the candles and turn off whatever lights you don't want on, but let at least one candle burn itself out.

—Magenta Griffith

5 Saturday
4th ♐
☽ v/c 8:07 am
☽ enters ♑ 9:32 am
Color: Gray

6 Sunday
4th ♑
♂ enters ♑ 1:32 pm
☽ v/c 8:47 pm
Color: Orange

As a familiar, the magpie teaches
the reading of signs and omens

February

7 Monday
4th ♑
☽ enters ♒ 9:26 am
Color: Lavender

Death of Thomas Aquinas, scholar who
wrote that heresy was a product of
ignorance and therefore criminal, and
who refuted the *Canon Episcopi*, 1274

 Tuesday
4th ♒
New Moon 5:28 pm
☽ v/c 11:19 pm
Color: Maroon

Mardi Gras
Birthday of Susun Weed, owner of
Wise Woman Publishing
Birthday of Evangeline Adams,
American astrologer, 1868

9 Wednesday
1st ♒
☽ enters ♓ 8:59 am
Color: Yellow

Ash Wednesday
Chinese New Year (rooster)

10 Thursday
1st ♓
Color: White

Islamic New Year
Zsusanna Budapest arrested and later
convicted for fortunetelling, 1975

11 Friday
1st ♓
☽ v/c 12:14 am
☽ enters ♈ 10:21 am
☿ enters ♓ 11:07 am
Color: Rose

February

February begins with the sabbat of the Irish goddess Brigid, ruler of fire, inspiration, and sovereignty. The winter will start to wane throughout the month, leading us to a rebirth in the spring.

In many places the February Sun is still cocooned in deep winter. The New Moon of February 8 can help us remember that the warmth of spring will indeed return. The New Moon is about beginnings, and by honoring her we reaffirm our connection to the God, Goddess, Moon, Sun, and Earth.

Mark the five pentacle points around you. Before you start to walk to each point, light a single candle. Be sure it's a safe candle—one that won't burn your hands, drop wax onto carpets, or topple and cause a fire. At each point say:

> *Earth of winter, unawakened still,*
> *Stir to the coming spring, we will.*
> *The Goddess and God, their blessings flow,*
> *Through Sun and Moon to us below.*

—Edain McCoy

12 Saturday
1st ♈
Color: Brown

Gerald Gardner, founder of the Gardnerian tradition, dies of heart failure, 1964

13 Sunday
1st ♈
☽ v/c 5:53 am
☽ enters ♉ 3:18 pm
Color: Gold

To gain extra power, eat ginger before performing a spell—especially a love spell

February

14 Monday
1st ♉
Color: Silver

Valentine's Day
Elsie Blum, a farmhand from
Oberstedten, Germany, sentenced
to death for witchcraft, 1652

○ Tuesday
1st ♉
2nd Quarter 7:16 pm
☽ v/c 10:07 pm
Color: Gray

Pope Leo X issues bull to ensure that the
secular courts carry out executions of
Witches convicted by the Inquisition,
1521; the bull was a response to the courts'
refusal to carry out the work of the Church

16 Wednesday
2nd ♉
☽ enters ♊ 12:18 am
☿ enters ♓ 12:46 pm
Color: White

*Wear silver to bolster your psychic
abilities; it's a receptive metal and will help
you receive psychic impressions more easily*

17 Thursday
2nd ♊
Color: Turquoise

18 Friday
2nd ♊
☽ v/c 12:23 am
☉ enters ♓ 8:32 am
☽ enters ♋ 12:13 pm
Color: Coral

Sun enters Pisces
Celtic Tree Month of Ash begins

19 Saturday
2nd ♋
Color: Blue

20 Sunday
2nd ♋
☽ v/c 7:06 am
Color: Yellow

Society for Psychical Research,
devoted to paranormal research,
founded in London, 1882

February

21 Monday

2nd ♋
☽ enters ♌ 12:54 am
♀ enters ♒ 12:39 pm
Color: Ivory

Presidents' Day (observed)
Birthday of Patricia Telesco,
Wiccan author
Stewart Farrar initiated into
Alexandrian Wicca, 1970
Death of Theodore Parker Mills, 1996

22 Tuesday

2nd ♌
Color: Scarlet

Birthday of ShadowCat, Wiccan author
Birthday of Sybil Leek, Wiccan author, 1922

☺ Wednesday

2nd ♌
☽ v/c 4:47 am
☽ enters ♍ 12:44 pm
Full Moon 11:54 pm
Color: Topaz

Quickening Moon

24 Thursday

3rd ♍
Color: Purple

25 Friday

3rd ♍
☽ v/c 12:00 pm
☽ enters ♎ 10:59 pm
Color: White

*Eggs represent fertility and life; colored
eggs mimic the returning flowers of spring*

Set in Eastern Standard Time (EST)

The Functions of Love

Love links magic to mindfulness,
Reminding us to care for each other.
It laughs in the face of fear,
And unfreezes fate into freedom.

Reminding us to care for each other,
Love links flesh to spirit
And unfreezes fate into freedom.
It draws us down into moonlight.

Love links flesh to spirit.
It laughs in the face of fear
And draws us down into moonlight.
Love links magic to mindfulness.

—Elizabeth Barrette

26 Saturday

3rd ♎
♀ enters ♓ 10:07 am
Color: Black

Oil of orange creates an uplifting, positive
atmosphere and is ideal for treating head colds

27 Sunday

3rd ♎
☽ v/c 8:49 pm
Color: Amber

Pope John XXII issues first bull to discuss
the practice of witchcraft, 1318
Birthday of Rudolph Steiner,
philosopher and father of the
biodynamic farming movement, 1861

28 Monday
3rd ♎
☽ enters ♏ 7:21 am
Color: Gray

Place a four-leaf clover in your lover's shoe to
help him or her remain faithful while traveling

1 Tuesday
3rd ♏
Color: Red

Preliminary hearings in the
Salem Witch trials held, 1692
Birthday of the Golden Dawn, 1888
Covenant of the Goddess (COG) formed, 1975

2 Wednesday
3rd ♏
☽ v/c 5:25 am
☽ enters ♐ 1:29 pm
Color: Yellow

◖ Thursday
3rd ♐
4th Quarter 12:36 pm
Color: Green

4 Friday
4th ♐
☽ v/c 4:45 pm
☽ enters ♑ 5:12 pm
☿ enters ♈ 8:34 pm
Color: Pink

Church of All Worlds incorporates in
Missouri, 1968, becoming the first Pagan
church to incorporate in the U.S.

Fancy Frittata

1 onion, diced
1 or 2 cloves of garlic, diced fine
1 cup mushrooms, sliced
1 lb. bulk pork sausage (or hot
    Italian sausage)
1 16 oz. can tomatoes with Italian
    seasoning, drained and diced
1 cup Parmesan cheese, freshly grated
6 eggs, well beaten

Sauté onion, garlic, and mushrooms together in a medium cast-iron skillet.
Add sausage and brown. Drain the sausage, then pour tomatoes over the
sausage, stir, and heat until bubbling. Sprinkle ½ cup of Parmesan cheese
over mixture. Pour eggs over all and sprinkle with remaining cheese. Place
uncovered in the oven at 350 degrees for 25 to 30 minutes. Serve with a
hearty bread such as foccacia.

—ShadowCat

5 Saturday
4th ♑
Color: Brown

When you and a friend must part, exchange a
pair of garnets to ensure that you meet again

6 Sunday
4th ♑
☽ v/c 3:28 am
☽ enters ♒ 6:49 pm
Color: Gold

Birthday of Laurie Cabot, Wiccan author

March

7 Monday

4th ≈≈
Color: Lavender

William Butler Yeats initiated
into the Isis-Urania Temple
of the Golden Dawn, 1890

8 Tuesday

4th ≈≈
☽ v/c 10:28 am
☽ enters ♓ 7:32 pm
Color: Black

9 Wednesday

4th ♓
Color: Brown

Add dill seeds to your bath to make yourself irresistible

☽ Thursday

4th ♓
New Moon 4:10 am
☽ v/c 11:44 am
☽ enters ♈ 9:03 pm
Color: Purple

Date recorded for first meeting of
Dr. John Dee and Edward Kelly, 1582

Dutch clairvoyant and psychic
healer Gerard Croiser born, 1909

11 Friday

1st ♈
Color: Rose

*Adding a quartz crystal point to any stone spell
increases the power of the other stones and the charm itself*

Set in Eastern Standard Time (EST)

12 Saturday
1st ♈
☽ v/c 3:13 pm
Color: Gray

Stewart Edward White, psychic
researcher, born, 1873; he later
became president of the
American Society for Psychical
Research in San Francisco

13 Sunday
1st ♈
☽ enters ♉ 1:05 am
Color: Yellow

March

14 Monday
1st ♉
Color: Gray

Jacques de Molay, head of the
Knights Templar in France, retracts
his confession of heresy before being
burned at the stake, 1314

15 Tuesday
1st ♉
☽ v/c 1:10 am
☽ enters ♊ 8:44 am
Color: Maroon

Pete Pathfinder Davis becomes the first
Wiccan priest elected as president of the
Interfaith Council of Washington State, 1995

16 Wednesday
1st ♊
Color: White

◑ Thursday
1st ♊
2nd Quarter 2:19 pm
☽ v/c 2:19 pm
☽ enters ♋ 7:44 pm
Color: Turquoise

St. Patrick's Day
Eleanor Shaw and Mary Phillips executed
in England for bewitching a woman
and her two children, 1705

18 Friday
2nd ♋
Color: Coral

Celtic Tree Month of Alder begins
Birthday of Edgar Cayce, psychic researcher, 1877

Set in Eastern Standard Time (EST)

Ostara

I n the old days, you couldn't do much cleaning in the winter, so as soon as the weather began to warm and the snow began to melt, it was time to start scrubbing. Turning the whole house or apartment inside out and getting everything spotless is still a good idea. If your house isn't physically clean, it's harder to keep it psychically clean.

You can start by magically blessing your broom and other cleaning tools with salt and water. Take a small dish of salt, draw the sign of the pentagram over it and say, "I bless this salt." Then bless a cup of water the same way. Take three pinches of salt from the dish and put them in the water. Stir clockwise with your right hand. Sprinkle a few drops on your regular broom, saying, "I bless this broom that my life may be clean." Then sweep your house from top to bottom, and then out the back door. Then go through and open all the windows. Last, open the back door (or if you don't have a back door, the window furthest away from the door) and shout, "Begone dirt, begone cold, begone winter!" Then go to the front door and chant, "Welcome, welcome, thrice welcome spring."

—Magenta Griffith

19 Saturday

2nd ♋
☿ ℞ 7:13 pm
Color: Blue

Elizabethan statute against witchcraft enacted, 1563; this statute was replaced in 1604 by a stricter one from King James I

20 Sunday

2nd ♋
☉ enters ♈ 7:33 am
☽ v/c 7:59 am
☽ enters ♌ 8:17 am
♂ enters ♒ 1:02 pm
Color: Amber

Palm Sunday
Ostara/Spring Equinox
Sun enters Aries
International Astrology Day
Death of Lady Sheba, author
of *The Book of Shadows*, 2002

March

21 Monday
2nd ♌
☿ ℞ 4:29 am
♄ D 9:54 pm
Color: Silver

Mandate of Henry VIII against witchcraft enacted, 1542; repealed in 1547

Green Egg magazine founded, 1968

22 Tuesday
2nd ♌
☽ v/c 9:20 am
♀ enters ♈ 11:25 am
☽ enters ♍ 8:10 pm
Color: White

Pope Clement urged by Phillip IV
to suppress Templar order, 1311

23 Wednesday
2nd ♍
Color: Topaz

24 Thursday
2nd ♍
☽ v/c 7:36 pm
Color: Crimson

Birthday of Alyson Hannigan, who played
Willow on *Buffy the Vampire Slayer*

Arrest of Florence Newton, one of the
few Witches burned in Ireland, 1661

☺ Friday
2nd ♍
☽ enters ♎ 6:00 am
⚥ enters ♉ 10:38 am
Full Moon 3:58 pm
Color: White

Purim

Good Friday

Storm Moon

Innocent III issues bull to
establish the Inquisition, 1199

Set in Eastern Standard Time (EST)

March

This March we have the opportunity for a lengthy and lively spring Ostara. This year our equinox falls on the 20th, but our March Full Moon falls on the 25th—the date of the old Roman New Year.

The arrival of the spring should be greeted with joyous music and dance. We're moving from a frozen world into one in which animals, crops, people, and our mythic figures merge to create the world anew.

Spiral dancing is popular in spring rites. Everyone should bring tambourines, drums, rain sticks, castanets, etc. Let the leader set the rhythm of the dance. When the leader is tired, he or she should move to the back of the line and allow the next person to take his or her place. Dancers become so entranced in rhythmic dance that all sense of time and space disappear as this unique esbat connects lunar and solar energy.

—Edain McCoy

26 Saturday

3rd ♎
☿ R⃯ 9:29 pm
Color: Indigo

Birthday of Joseph Campbell, author
and professor of mythology, 1910

27 Sunday

3rd ♎
☽ v/c 3:30 am
☽ enters ♏ 1:29 pm
Color: Orange

Easter

March/April

28 Monday

3rd ♏
Color: Ivory

Scott Cunningham dies of
complications caused by AIDS, 1993

29 Tuesday
3rd ♏
☽ v/c 2:06 am
☽ enters ♐ 6:56 pm
Color: Scarlet

Tulips are aligned with the element of earth;
they encourage good luck and prosperity

30 Wednesday

3rd ♐
Color: Brown

31 Thursday

3rd ♐
☽ v/c 1:24 pm
☿ enters ♍ 9:55 pm
☽ enters ♑ 10:48 pm
Color: White

Last Witch trial in Ireland,
held at Magee Island, 1711

☽ Friday

3rd ♑
4th Quarter 7:50 pm
Color: Purple

April Fools' Day

54   *Set in Eastern Standard Time (EST)*

April

Though not an "official" Pagan holiday, April Fools' Day has been around for about three hundred years. The Moon slips in to April near the end of its Sagittarius transit, and that energy will provide a boost for pranksters who are ambitious, exuberant, and don't mind taking a walk on the wild side once in a while.

This is a holiday when the Lord of Misrule (who later became the "court jester" to European royalty) and his bride Discordia rule the world, wreaking havoc and enjoying all tricks that harm no one. As you set up a joke or trick on someone, ask the Lord of Misrule and Discordia to cause your prank to go as planned, and that no one be harmed by April Fools' fun.

—Edain McCoy

2 Saturday
4th ♑
☽ v/c 9:34 am
Color: Gray

*Give catnip to your feline familiar; it will
create a psychic bond between the two of you*

3 Sunday
4th ♑
☽ enters ♒ 1:31 am
Color: Amber

Daylight Saving Time begins at 2 am

April

4 Monday
4th ≈
☽ v/c 7:32 pm
Color: Silver

*Ranging in color from delicate pink to lavender, the
stone kunzite relieves stress, especially in the workplace*

5 Tuesday
4th ≈
☽ enters ♓ 4:45 am
Color: Red

Trial of Alice Samuel, her
husband, and daughter, who
were accused of bewitching the
wife of Sir Henry Cromwell and
several village children, 1593

6 Wednesday
4th ♓
☽ v/c 10:03 pm
Color: Yellow

7 Thursday
4th ♓
☽ enters ♈ 7:28 am
Color: Green

Church of All Worlds founded, 1962
First Wiccan "tract" published
by Pete Pathfinder Davis, 1996

 Friday
4th ♈
New Moon 4:32 pm
Color: Coral

Solar eclipse 4:37 pm, 19° ♈ 06'

William Alexander Aynton initiated into
the Isis-Urania temple of the Golden
Dawn, 1896; he would later be called the
"Grand Old Man" of the Golden Dawn

Set in Eastern Daylight Time (EDT)

The Sources of Power

Power is as much a part of us as air—
Never seen, but ever sensed and always there.
It fills us up as we breathe out and breathe in,
Dancing in swift goosebumps over
    quickened skin.
It empties us when we've borne too much
    to bear.

It rises like sap through branches winter-bare,
Bursting forth in leaves and blossoms
    summer-fair.
A fountain of wonder coming from within,
Power is.

It flows like rivers that the oceans ensnare,
Running from each to other, following care.
To lead is to lie beneath, gathering in
The streams that come from without, that slip and spin.
A peculiar dance of give and take and share,
Power is.

                      —Elizabeth Barrette

---

9 Saturday

1st ♈
☽ v/c 2:00 am
☽ enters ♉ 11:50 am
Color: Blue

---

10 Sunday

1st ♉
Color: Orange

Birthday of Rev. Montague Summers,
orthodox scholar and author of *A
History of Witchcraft and Demonology*, 1880

April

11 Monday

1st ♉
☽ v/c 1:37 am
☽ enters ♊ 6:55 pm
Color: Lavender

Burning of Major Weir, Scottish "sorcerer" who confessed of his own accord, 1670; some historians believe that the major became delusional or senile because up until his confession he had an excellent reputation and was a pillar of society

12 Tuesday

1st ♊
☿ D 3:45 am
Color: White

Handfasting of Oberon and Morning Glory Zell, 1974

13 Wednesday

1st ♊
⚳ enters ♈ 8:29 pm
Color: Brown

First confession of witchcraft by Isobel Gowdie, whose case is considered unusual because no torture was used to extract her confession, Scotland, 1662

14 Thursday

1st ♊
☽ v/c 1:01 am
☽ enters ♋ 5:03 am
Color: Crimson

Adoption of the Principles of Wiccan Belief at "Witch Meet" in St. Paul, Minnesota, 1974

15 Friday

1st ♋
♀ enters ♉ 4:37 pm
Color: Pink

Celtic Tree Month of Willow begins
Birthday of Elizabeth Montgomery, who played Samantha on *Bewitched*, 1933

☽ Saturday

1st ♋
2nd Quarter 10:37 am
☽ v/c 10:37 am
☽ enters ♌ 5:17 pm
Color: Indigo

Birthday of Margot Adler, author
of *Drawing Down the Moon*

17 Sunday

2nd ♌
Color: Yellow

Aleister Crowley breaks into and takes over the
Golden Dawn temple, providing the catalyst for
the demise of the original Golden Dawn, 1900

April

18 Monday
2nd ♌
Color: Gray

Gather the first violets of the spring and fashion them into a little posy; this encourages love and fairy magic

19 Tuesday
2nd ♌
☽ v/c 4:13 am
☽ enters ♍ 5:27 am
☉ enters ♉ 7:37 pm
Color: Scarlet

Sun enters Taurus
Conviction of Witches at second of four famous trials at Chelmsford, England, 1579

20 Wednesday
2nd ♍
Color: White

21 Thursday
2nd ♍
☽ v/c 4:45 am
☽ enters ♎ 3:27 pm
Color: Purple

Adding a few tumbled semiprecious stones to your garden encourages the benevolence of the nature spirits and fairies

22 Friday
2nd ♎
Color: Rose

Earth Day; the first Earth Day was in 1970

Set in Eastern Daylight Time (EDT)

Lunar Eclipse

A lunar eclipse has two phases with opposing energies. The first phase is to obscure or hide that which we don't want anyone else to see, including one's self. We all have a dark side, or a shadow self, which we can access with the help of a lunar eclipse.

As the Earth's shadow begins to obscure the face of the Moon, close your eyes and lower your head into your lap or onto the ground. Focus on your dark side—the shadow self you must meet and integrate into yourself to both understand yourself and to be a whole being.

Feel the Earth's shadow covering you. Visualize the darkening Moon showing you the hidden aspects of yourself you need to know. Be aware that not all of them are flattering, but they are a part of you.

When you feel the light of the Full Moon shining down on you once again, raise your head and thank the Moon. Record your experiences while they are fresh in your mind.

—Edain McCoy

23 Saturday

2nd ♎︎
☽ v/c 12:46 pm
☽ enters ♏︎ 10:25 pm
Color: Brown

Edward III of England begins the
Order of the Garter, 1350
First National All-Woman Conference on
Women's Spirituality held, Boston, 1976

☺ Sunday

2nd ♏︎
Full Moon 6:06 am
Color: Gold

Passover begins
Wind Moon
Lunar eclipse 5:56 am, 4° ♏︎ 20'

25 Monday

3rd ♏
☽ v/c 8:24 pm
Color: Ivory

USA Today reports that Patricia Hutchins is
the first military Wiccan granted religious
leave for the sabbats, 1989

26 Tuesday

3rd ♏
☽ enters ♐ 2:46 am
Color: Black

*Tuck a sprig of rosemary beneath your pillow to
promote restful sleep and sweet untroubled dreams*

27 Wednesday

3rd ♐
Color: Topaz

Carry dice in your pocket for good luck

28 Thursday

3rd ♐
☽ v/c 2:02 am
☽ enters ♑ 5:33 am
Color: Turquoise

29 Friday

3rd ♑
☽ v/c 6:00 pm
Color: White

Orthodox Good Friday
Birthday of Ed Fitch, Wiccan author

Beltane

Beltane is experienced differently by different people, depending on whether they are single or not. If you do have a mate or partner, this is a good time to celebrate the relationship. Each of you should make a list of seven qualities you most appreciate and cherish in the other. These should be inherent traits, like a sense of humor, or being good with animals. Do this separately a few days before Beltane.

On May Eve, draw a circle, if you wish, in whatever fashion you usually do. Then sit facing each other, holding hands. You might want to do this sitting on your bed. One of you starts by saying "I love you because . . ." naming one of the qualities previously listed. (You can flip a coin to decide who goes first.) Then the other one does the same, alternating down through the list. When you are finished, say together, "I love you because you are *you!*" Finish with a kiss. If you are alone on Beltane you can make a list of qualities you like about yourself. Do this ritual in front of a mirror, saying what you love about yourself, to yourself.

—Magenta Griffith

---

30 Saturday

3rd ♑
☽ enters ♒ 7:54 am
♂ enters ♓ 10:58 pm
Color: Blue

Passover ends
Walpurgis Night; traditionally the
German Witches gather on the Blocksberg,
a mountain in northeastern Germany

◖ Sunday

3rd ♒
4th Quarter 2:24 am
Color: Orange

Orthodox Easter
Beltane/May Day
Order of the Illuminati formed in
Bavaria by Adam Weishaupt, 1776

May

2 Monday
4th ≈
☽ v/c 12:47 am
☽ enters ✕ 10:43 am
Color: Gray

Deep blue lapis lazuli promotes
loyalty, fidelity, and spiritual thoughts

3 Tuesday
4th ✕
Color: Red

Birthday of D. J. Conway, Wiccan author

4 Wednesday
4th ✕
☽ v/c 4:22 am
☽ enters ♈ 2:36 pm
Color: Yellow

The *New York Herald Tribune*
carries the story of a woman who
brought her neighbor to court on
a charge of bewitchment, 1895

5 Thursday
4th ♈
Color: Purple

Cinco de Mayo
Beltane crossquarter day
(Sun reaches 15° Taurus)

6 Friday
4th ♈
☽ v/c 9:22 am
☽ enters ♉ 8:01 pm
Color: Pink

Long Island Church of Aphrodite
formed by Reverend Gleb Botkin, 1938

May

M ay 1 comes carrying a perfect waning crescent Moon, full of energy that can be tapped for things you wish to change.

Under the May 1 Moon, begin focusing on that which you want but do not have. When the New Moon comes around on the 8th, begin to focus all your energies on attainment. For example, if you're short of money, visualize having all you need before the month ends.

The Moon will be full on the 24th. On this night visualize yourself having what you want and need, and that you got it without harm to others. Visualize yourself immersed in the imagery of your spell—for example, imagine money in your bank account physically growing to cover your needs and goals.

—Edain McCoy

7 Saturday
4th ♉
Color: Indigo

☽ Sunday

4th ♉
New Moon 4:45 am
☿ ℞ 9:47 pm
Color: Yellow

Mother's Day

May

9 Monday

1st ♉
☽ v/c 1:15 am
☽ enters ♊ 3:29 am
Color: Lavender

Joan of Arc canonized, 1920
First day of the Lemuria, a Roman
festival of the dead; this festival
was probably borrowed from the
Etruscans and is one possible
ancestor of our modern Halloween

10 Tuesday

1st ♊
♀ enters ♊ 12:14 am
Color: White

11 Wednesday

1st ♊
☽ v/c 10:58 am
☽ enters ♋ 1:20 pm
☿ D 9:45 pm
Color: Brown

Massachusetts Bay Colony Puritans
ban Christmas celebrations
because they are too pagan, 1659

12 Thursday

1st ♋
☿ enters ♉ 5:13 am
Color: Green

To attract the fairies to your shady garden, plant
violets, lady's mantle, ferns, foxgloves, and bluebells

13 Friday

1st ♋
☽ v/c 11:04 am
Color: Rose

Celtic Tree Month of Hawthorn begins

Set in Eastern Daylight Time (EDT)

A Reflection of Father Time

Slowly the Great Wheel turns around,
Marking the seasons of the year:
Summer ripens to Autumn's red,
Winter gives way to blooming spring.
Holidays come, holidays go;
Slowly the Great Wheel turns around.
Labors give fruit, and we give praise,
Watching legacies grow like grain.
Families flourish, careers as well;
Our spirits deepen in our craft.
Slowly the Great Wheel turns around,
Calling us home to Summerland.
We leave the fields that we have hoed
To walk the hills with Father Time
Till our souls dream once more of spring . . .
Slowly the Great Wheel turns around.
                              —Elizabeth Barrette

14 Saturday
1st ♋
☽ enters ♌ 1:17 am
Color: Gray

Widow Robinson of Kidderminster
and her two daughters are arrested for
trying to prevent the return of Charles II
from exile by use of magic, 1660

15 Sunday
1st ♌
Color: Gold

May

☽ Monday
1st ♌
2nd Quarter 4:57 am
☽ v/c 4:57 am
☽ enters ♍ 1:46 pm
Color: White

To attract the fairies to your sunny garden, plant
yarrow, roses, rue, betony, lavender, and morning glory

17 Tuesday
2nd ♍
Color: Black

18 Wednesday
2nd ♍
☽ v/c 9:00 pm
Color: Topaz

19 Thursday
2nd ♍
☽ enters ♎ 12:30 am
♆ ℞ 7:36 pm
Color: Turquoise

A Full Moon in May is a sacred time to bless your magical
garden, flowers, herbs, plants, and enchanting trees

20 Friday
2nd ♎
☉ enters ∏ 6:47 pm
☽ v/c 8:40 pm
Color: Coral

Sun enters Gemini

Set in Eastern Daylight Time (EDT)

Love on a Bun Porketta

¼ cup fennel seeds
¼ cup onion, chopped
5 cloves garlic
2 tbs. salt
2 tbs. ground pepper
¼ cup olive oil
3 to 5 lb. pork shoulder roast,
    deboned and butterflied
Cotton kitchen string

Put fennel, onion, garlic, salt, pepper, and olive oil in food processor and blend until mixture is a spreadable paste. Add more olive oil as needed.

Wash the pork roast and pat dry. Open the roast and spread half the mixture on the inside layers of roast. Fold the roast closed and tie with three pieces of string so the roast will remain closed while cooking. Spread the remaining mixture over the entire roast. Wrap roast in plastic wrap and refrigerate overnight. Either roast in the oven at 350 degrees for 2½ to 3 hours in a roasting pan or place in a crockpot on low setting for 10 to 12 hours. Porketta is traditionally served on hard rolls, but, for a crowd, hamburger buns are fine. Serve with potato salad and coleslaw.

—ShadowCat

21 Saturday

2nd ♎︎
☽ enters ♏︎ 7:49 am
Color: Blue

Birthday of Gwyddion Pendderwen,
Pagan bard, 1946

22 Sunday

2nd ♏︎
Color: Amber

Adoption of the Earth Religion
Anti-Abuse Act, 1988

May

☺ Monday
2nd ♏
☽ v/c 12:54 am
☽ enters ♐ 11:38 am
Full Moon 4:18 pm
Color: Silver

Flower Moon

24 Tuesday
3rd ♐
Color: Gray

The Chinese carve jade butterflies to exchange as love tokens

25 Wednesday
3rd ♐
☽ v/c 2:52 am
☽ enters ♑ 1:11 pm
Color: White

Scott Cunningham initiated into
the Traditional Gwyddonic
Order of the Wicca, 1981

26 Thursday
3rd ♑
Color: Crimson

27 Friday
3rd ♑
☽ v/c 11:22 am
☽ enters ♒ 2:10 pm
Color: Purple

Birthday of Morning Glory
Zell, Church of All Worlds

Final confession of witchcraft by
Isobel Gowdie, Scotland, 1662

Set in Eastern Daylight Time (EDT)

28 Saturday

3rd ≈
☿ enters ♊ 6:44 am
Color: Brown

For best results, plant annual flowers in the waxing Moon
and perennial flowers, trees, and shrubs in the waning Moon

29 Sunday

3rd ≈
☽ v/c 5:19 am
☽ enters ♓ 4:09 pm
Color: Orange

May/June

○ Monday
3rd ♓
4th Quarter 7:47 am
Color: Ivory

Memorial Day (observed)
Death of Joan of Arc, 1431

31 Tuesday
4th ♓
☽ v/c 1:53 pm
☽ enters ♈ 8:07 pm
Color: Maroon

1 Wednesday
4th ♈
♅ enters ♊ 12:31 pm
Color: Yellow

Witchcraft Act of 1563
takes effect in England

2 Thursday
4th ♈
Color: Turquoise

Birthday of Alessandro
di Cagliostro, magician, 1743

3 Friday
4th ♈
☽ v/c 1:24 am
☽ enters ♉ 2:20 am
♀ enters ♋ 11:18 am
Color: White

Crumbled and dried betony (lamb's ears)
sprinkled around the perimeter of your home
creates a protective boundary and promotes security

Set in Eastern Daylight Time (EDT)

In Honor of Mother Earth

As Her body is our body,
From bone of rock to blood of brine,
There can be no true division
Between the people and the land.
We see ourselves in all the world.
As Her body is our body,
From breath of wind to kiss of rain,
We speak with Her words and Her voice.
She is our first inspiration,
Our second nature, our last hope.
As Her body is our body,
From seed of grain to womb of field,
Our joys and griefs return to us.
Pledging ourselves to Her service,
We only reap what we have sown
For Her body is our body.

—Elizabeth Barrette

---

4 Saturday

4th ♉
Color: Indigo

---

5 Sunday

4th ♉
☽ v/c 1:25 am
♃ D 3:20 am
☽ enters ♊ 10:36 am
Color: Orange

☽ Monday
4th ♊
New Moon 5:55 pm
Color: Gray

Hematite heals by drawing illness out of the body

7 Tuesday
1st ♊
☽ v/c 2:50 pm
☽ enters ♋ 8:46 pm
Color: White

8 Wednesday
1st ♋
Color: Brown

*Gather flowers for charms and spells early in the
cool of the morning; they will stay fresh longer*

9 Thursday
1st ♋
Color: Crimson

Birthday of Grace Cook, medium and
founder of the White Eagle Lodge, 1892

10 Friday
1st ♋
☽ v/c 6:18 am
☽ enters ♌ 8:39 am
Color: Pink

Celtic Tree Month of Oak begins

Hanging of Bridget Bishop, first to
die in the Salem Witch trials, 1692

June

We tend to think of homey celebrations as being wintertime events, but the Sun moving into Cancer and the Moon aspecting it this month make a potent energy for any spell associated with home, family, peace, and love.

Collect dried herbs or flowers associated with love and peace, such as rue, basil, lotus, yarrow, or myrtle.

On the morning of June 9, walk clockwise around the perimeter of your home. As you scatter the herbs say:

Around my home the bane is gone,
Blocked from entry by my song.
Bane inside does flee, it must,
Taking with it all negative dust.
I court the host of the spirits of love,
Such as the deities up above.
A mantle of protection three times three,
By my will, so mote it be.

—Edain McCoy

---

11 Saturday

1st ♌
☿ enters ♋ 3:03 am
♂ enters ♈ 10:30 pm
✳ enters ♉ 10:30 pm
Color: Blue

James I Witchcraft Statute replaces the
1563 mandate with stricter penalties, 1604

---

12 Sunday

1st ♌
☽ v/c 7:40 am
☽ enters ♍ 9:22 pm
Color: Gold

June

13 Monday
1st ♍
Color: Ivory

Shavuot

Birthday of William Butler Yeats, poet
and member of the Golden Dawn, 1865

Birthday of Gerald Gardner, founder
of the Gardnerian Tradition, 1884

◐ Tuesday
1st ♍
♅ ℞ 6:38 pm
2nd Quarter 9:22 pm
Color: Black

Flag Day

15 Wednesday
2nd ♍
☽ v/c 1:24 am
☽ enters ♎ 8:59 am
Color: White

Margaret Jones becomes the first person executed
as a Witch in the Massachusetts Bay Colony,
1648; she was a Boston doctor who was accused of
witchcraft after several of her patients died

16 Thursday
2nd ♎
Color: Green

17 Friday
2nd ♎
☽ v/c 11:02 am
☽ enters ♏ 5:23 pm
Color: Rose

Birthday of Starhawk, Wiccan author

Set in Eastern Daylight Time (EDT)

18 Saturday

2nd ♏

Color: Gray

Church of All Worlds
chartered with the IRS, 1970

19 Sunday

2nd ♏

☽ v/c 4:06 pm

☽ enters ♐ 9:45 pm

Color: Amber

Pentecost

Father's Day

Birthday of James I of England,
famous for his anti-witchcraft laws, 1566

20 Monday
2nd ♐
Color: Silver

21 Tuesday
2nd ♐
☉ enters ♋ 2:46 am
☽ v/c 11:34 am
☽ enters ♑ 10:52 pm
Color: Gray

Midsummer/Litha/Summer Solstice
Sun enters Cancer

☺ Wednesday

2nd ♑
Full Moon 12:14 am
Color: Topaz

Strong Sun Moon
Final witchcraft law in
England repealed, 1951

23 Thursday

3rd ♑
☽ v/c 6:04 pm
☽ enters ♒ 10:36 pm
Color: Crimson

24 Friday

3rd ♒
Color: Purple

Birthday of Janet Farrar, Wiccan author
James I Witchcraft Statute of 1604 is
replaced in 1763 with a law against
pretending to practice divination and
witchcraft; law stands until 1951

Litha

The Summer Solstice, the zenith of the Sun, is an excellent time to do spells for abundance and prosperity. Take three green candles and three gold or bright yellow candles and put them in gold-colored or brass candlesticks. Arrange them in a circle on your altar or on a table, alternating the colors. In the center of the candles, arrange money and symbols of money. Coins are good, for example, and dollar coins work especially well because they are gold colored. You might also put pictures or drawings of what form you want your abundance to take, like a new car, a bill paid, or stocks and bonds and other symbols of wealth and security.

Cast a circle as you usually would. Then chant, "Sun so high, bring me your bounty, warmth, and prosperity, bring me success. Bring me the means to fulfill my desires, enough and some to share." Repeat this chant and imagine the pile of coins on the altar growing, and the pictures and symbols becoming real. Hold the thought as long as you can, and as soon as your attention begins to waver, say, "So mote it be," and quickly blow out all the candles. End the circle in your usual manner.

—Magenta Griffith

---

25 Saturday

3rd ≈
☽ v/c 11:23 am
☽ enters ♓ 11:03 pm
Color: Brown

A law is introduced in Germany by Archbishop Siegfried III to encourage conversion rather than burning of heretics, 1233

---

26 Sunday

3rd ♓
☿ D 8:27 am
☿ enters ♎ 7:04 pm
Color: Yellow

Birthday of Stewart Farrar, Wiccan author

Richard of Gloucester assumes the English throne after accusing the widowed queen of Edward IV of witchcraft, 1483

June/July

27 Monday

3rd ♓
Color: Lavender

Birthday of Scott Cunningham,
Wiccan author, 1956

○ Tuesday
3rd ♓
☿ enters ♌ 12:01 am
☽ v/c 1:51 am
☽ enters ♈ 1:51 am
♀ enters ♌ 1:53 am
4th Quarter 2:23 pm
Color: Scarlet

*Made of fossilized tree resin,
amber holds the power of the Sun*

29 Wednesday
4th ♈
Color: Brown

30 Thursday
4th ♈
☽ v/c 3:57 am
☽ enters ♉ 7:45 am
Color: Purple

1 Friday
4th ♉
Color: Coral

*Ozark folklore tells us that when a honey bee
flies around your head, money is on the way*

Set in Eastern Daylight Time (EDT)

A Song for Solidarity

I am one howl in a serenade.
I am one note in a summer song,
And one face of which the pack is made.

Gray brothers are my strength, unafraid.
Gray sisters are my joy, bright and long.
I am one howl in a serenade.

I am one shape of the soul's cascade,
One body lost in the loving throng,
And one face of which the pack is made.

My magic's a descant overlaid
On our melody of evensong:
I am one howl in a serenade.

I am one leap in the hidden glade,
One resplendent spell spun out lifelong,
And one face of which the pack is made.

With solidarity I have paid
The circle to which all wolves belong.
I am one howl in a serenade,
And one face of which the pack is made.

—Elizabeth Barrette

---

2 Saturday
4th ♉
☽ v/c 1:02 pm
☽ enters ♊ 4:26 pm
Color: Gray

---

3 Sunday

4th ♊
Color: Orange

Trial of Joan Prentice, who was accused
of sending an imp in the form of a
ferret to bite children; she allegedly had
two imps named Jack and Jill, 1549

---

4 Monday
4th ♊
☽ v/c 12:36 pm
Color: White

Independence Day

5 Tuesday
4th ♊
☽ enters ♋ 3:07 am
Color: Maroon

Conviction of Witches at third of four
famous trials at Chelmsford, England, 1589

Wednesday
4th ♋
New Moon 8:02 am
Color: Yellow

Scott Cunningham is initiated into
the Ancient Pictish Gaelic Way, 1981

7 Thursday
1st ♋
☽ v/c 12:54 pm
☽ enters ♌ 3:11 pm
Color: Green

8 Friday
1st ♌
Color: White

Celtic Tree Month of Holly

Strawberry Rhubarb Pie

Pie Crust:
3 cups all purpose flour
½ lb. lard
½ cup cold milk
1 tsp. salt

Filling:
3 eggs, well beaten
1¼ cups sugar
¼ cup all-purpose flour
¼ tsp. salt
2½ cups rhubarb, cut in 1-inch pieces
1½ cups fresh strawberries, sliced
1 tbs. butter
½ tsp. nutmeg

Pie crust: Cut lard into flour and salt. Add milk and shape into two balls. Roll out into two pie crusts and line a 9-inch pan with one crust.
Filling: Mix eggs, sugar, flour, salt, and nutmeg together. Combine rhubarb and strawberries and place in pan. Pour egg mixture over the fruit and dot with butter. Top with second crust, crimping the edge high. Bake at 400 degrees for 40 minutes. Serve warm.

—ShadowCat

9 Saturday
1st ♌
☽ v/c 12:49 pm
Color: Indigo

Death of Herman Slater,
proprietor of Magickal Childe
bookstore in New York, 1992
Birthday of Amber K, Wiccan author

10 Sunday

1st ♌
☽ enters ♍ 3:57 am
Color: Amber

*Plant cherry-scented heliotrope in your sunny
gardens; believed to grant invisibility, they
help to ensure your privacy from neighbors*

July

11 Monday
1st ♍
Color: Gray

12 Tuesday
1st ♍
☽ v/c 3:12 pm
☽ enters ♎ 4:09 pm
Color: Red

13 Wednesday
1st ♎
Color: Brown

Birthday of Dr. John Dee, magician, 1527

◐ Thursday
1st ♎
2nd Quarter 11:20 am
Color: Turquoise

First crop circles recorded
on Silbury Hill, 1988

15 Friday
2nd ♎
☽ v/c 1:32 am
☽ enters ♏ 1:51 am
Color: Pink

16 Saturday

2nd ♏
♄ enters ♌ 8:30 am
☽ v/c 10:15 pm
Color: Blue

*Grow green beans in your garden; they
are sacred to the Goddess, and the blossom's
scent guides spirits to their resting place*

17 Sunday

2nd ♏
☽ enters ♐ 7:35 am
Color: Yellow

First airing of *The Witching Hour*, a
Pagan radio show hosted by Winter
Wren and Don Lewis, on station
WONX in Evanston, Illinois, 1992

18 Monday
2nd ♐
Color: Silver

19 Tuesday
2nd ♐
☽ v/c 2:03 am
☽ enters ♑ 9:26 am
Color: Black

Rebecca Nurse hanged in
Salem, Massachusetts, 1692

20 Wednesday
2nd ♑
Color: White

Pope Adrian VI issues a bull to the
Inquisition to re-emphasize the 1503
bull of Julius II calling for the purging
of "sorcerers by fire and sword," 1523

☺ Thursday
2nd ♑
Full Moon 7:00 am
☽ v/c 7:00 am
☽ enters ♒ 8:55 am
Color: Purple

Blessing Moon

22 Friday
3rd ♒
☉ enters ♌ 1:41 pm
♀ enters ♍ 9:01 pm
☿ ℞ 10:59 pm
Color: Rose

Sun enters Leo

Northamptonshire Witches
condemned, 1612

First modern recorded sighting
of the Loch Ness Monster, 1930

July

U ranus, Neptune, and Pluto will spend their July in retrograde. Because these planets reflect the world around us, we must look out for misunderstandings, wars, threats to the environment, and other potential crises.

You may beseech the maternal lunar energies to help quiet the roars and growls of a world in combat with itself. Gaze up at the night sky. Meditate for a moment on your purpose and visualize the world's horrors being erased by the silver glow of Mother Moon.

> Mother Moon, we call to you,
> You can do much more than we can do;
> Heal the Earth, its scars, its tears,
> So it may be here another thousand years.
> Heal the people of their hatred and ire,
> Call on the transformative element of fire,
> Guide us, Mother, to do what is right
> For your sacred Earth on which we stand tonight.

—Edain McCoy

---

23 Saturday

3rd ≈
☽ v/c 3:33 am
☽ enters ♓ 8:12 am
Color: Brown

To prevent nightmares, make a dreampillow stuffed with anise seeds

---

24 Sunday

3rd ♓
☽ v/c 8:19 pm
Color: Gold

July

25 Monday
3rd ♓
☽ enters ♈ 9:23 am
Color: Ivory

Death of Pope Innocent VIII, who issued
bull *Summis Desiderantes Affectibus*, 1492

26 Tuesday
3rd ♈
Color: White

Confession of Chelmsford Witches at first
of four famous trials at Chelmsford, 1566;
the others were held in 1579, 1589, and
1645; "Witch Finder General" Matthew
Hopkins presided at the 1645 trials

◗ Wednesday
3rd ♈
☽ v/c 1:23 pm
☽ enters ♉ 1:54 pm
4th Quarter 11:19 pm
Color: Topaz

Jennet Preston becomes the first of the
"Malkin Tower" Witches to be hung; she
was convicted of hiring Witches to help
her murder Thomas Lister, 1612

28 Thursday
4th ♉
♂ enters ♉ 1:12 am
Color: Crimson

Bake blackberry pies for Lughnasadh in honor of the dying God

29 Friday
4th ♉
☽ v/c 12:59 am
☽ enters ♊ 10:02 pm
Color: Purple

Agnes Waterhouse, one of the Chelmsford
Witches, is hanged under the new witchcraft
statute of Elizabeth I, 1566; she was accused of
having a spotted cat familiar named Sathan

Set in Eastern Daylight Time (EDT)

August

Leo is the royal ruler of the heavens. When the New Moon of August 4 joins the Sun in its transit through Leo, take advantage of the merging of two strong planets in a sign that explodes with self-confidence and immutable will. This transit can enhance the personality you want to show the world, and help you understand the Leonine lunar aspects hidden inside you.

At twilight, stop to contemplate the ways in which the attributes of Leo are integrated in you, and say:

> *Roaring Lion of the skies,*
> *Help to open my closed eyes.*
> *I want your heat, your heart, your fire,*
> *To show the world that I desire.*
> *And bless me too, dear New Moon hiding,*
> *Polarizing the aspects in me abiding.*
> *Give me the strength to integrate, too,*
> *The power of fire, I ask of you.*

—Edain McCoy

---

30 Saturday
4th ♊
Color: Black

Conrad of Marburg is murdered on the open road, presumably because he had shifted from persecuting poor heretics to nobles, 1233

---

31 Sunday
4th ♊
☽ v/c 5:10 pm
⚷ enters ♑ 11:39 pm
Color: Amber

Birthday of H. P. Blavatsky, founder of the Theosophical Society, 1831

Date of fabled meeting of British Witches to raise cone of power to stop Hitler's invasion of England, 1940

August

1 Monday

4th ♊
☽ enters ♋ 8:52 am
Color: Gray

Lammas/Lughnasadh
Birthday of Edward Kelly,
medium of Dr. John Dee, 1555
AURORA Network UK founded, 2000

2 Tuesday

4th ♋
☽ v/c 11:59 am
Color: Black

Birthday of Henry Steele Olcott,
who cofounded the Theosophical
Society with H. P. Blavatsky, 1832

3 Wednesday

4th ♋
☽ enters ♌ 9:10 pm
Color: Yellow

*Lavender is an herb of transformation; use this herb
to transform situations from negative to positive*

☽ Thursday

4th ♌
New Moon 11:05 pm
Color: Green

5 Friday

1st ♌
☽ v/c 5:45 pm
Color: White

Celtic Tree Month of Hazel begins

Set in Eastern Daylight Time (EDT)

Lughnasadh

Lughnasadh means "Lugh's games." It is traditionally the time when the Summer King is defeated by the Winter King, heralding the end of the warm, growing time of year and the advent of colder weather. At harvest fairs throughout the British Isles there were various games and mock battles to symbolize this. There were horse races, contests of strength and skill, and poetry competitions, as well as dancing and feasting.

A picnic with traditional games like tug-of-war, footraces, and relay races is an appropriate celebration of Lughnasadh. Include the children, and let them participate in the games as much as possible.

Once summer is defeated, a short period of mourning is called for—after all, summer is usually over too soon. Then should come the feast, featuring as much newly harvested food as possible. Bless the food before you eat:

Lugh, Lord of the Sun, Lord of Light,
Thank you for your bounty in this harvest,
Bless this food that we might share your strength.

—Magenta Griffith

---

6 Saturday

1st ♌
☽ enters ♍ 9:54 am
Color: Indigo

When a red bird (cardinal) crosses your path,
expect to receive a kiss before the day is out

---

7 Sunday

1st ♍
Color: Orange

Lammas crossquarter day
(Sun reaches 15° Leo)

August

8 Monday
1st ♍
☽ v/c 6:10 am
☽ enters ♎ 10:08 pm
Color: Lavender

*Lavender promotes calm, relieves insomnia, and
treats headaches—hence its use in linen closets*

9 Tuesday
1st ♎
Color: Gray

10 Wednesday
1st ♎
☽ v/c 5:10 pm
Color: Brown

11 Thursday
1st ♎
☽ enters ♏ 8:35 am
Color: Purple

Laurie Cabot withdraws from Salem,
Massachusetts, mayoral race, 1987
Birthday of Edain McCoy, Wiccan author

○ Friday
1st ♏
✳ enters ♊ 11:26 am
2nd Quarter 10.38 pm
Color: Pink

*Wearing bright blue bachelor's buttons—a
Venus flower—is thought to make you irresistible*

Set in Eastern Daylight Time (EDT)

A Meditation on Meaning

Search for meaning fills our days,
Trail of crumbs through thorny maze.
Still we show—a hidden clue—
Who we are through what we do.

Smoke and mirrors, truth and lies,
It should come as no surprise.
Deeds alone make our words true:
Who we are is what we do.

Thou are Goddess, so we say,
Choosing truth through roles we play
Making meaning from the skew:
Who we are and what we do.

—Elizabeth Barrette

13 Saturday
2nd ♏
♇ enters ♋ 6:45 am
☽ v/c 8:06 am
☽ enters ♐ 3:47 pm
Color: Black

Aradia de Toscano allegedly
born in Volterra, Italy, 1313
Church of Wicca founded in Australia
by Lady Tamara Von Forslun, 1989

14 Sunday
2nd ♐
Color: Amber

August

15 Monday
2nd ♐
☽ v/c 4:43 pm
☽ enters ♑ 7:13 pm
☿ D 11:49 pm
Color: Silver

Birthday of Charles Godfrey Leland,
author of *Aradia, Gospel of Witches*, 1824

16 Tuesday
2nd ♑
☽ v/c 9:02 pm
♀ enters ♎ 11:05 pm
Color: Red

17 Wednesday
2nd ♑
☽ enters ♒ 7:39 pm
Color: Topaz

Scott Cunningham's first
initiation into Wicca, 1973

18 Thursday
2nd ♒
Color: Turquoise

Father Urbain Grandier found
guilty of bewitching nuns at a
convent in Loudoun, France, 1634

☺ Friday
2nd ♒
Full Moon 1:53 pm
☽ v/c 1:53 pm
☽ enters ♓ 6:52 pm
Color: Coral

Corn Moon
John Willard and Reverend
George Burroughs put to death
in the Salem Witch trials, 1692

Set in Eastern Daylight Time (EDT)

Harvest Bread

2 eggs
½ cup butter
1 cup pumpkin, cooked
1 tsp. baking soda
1 tsp. salt
1 tsp. cinnamon
1 tsp. pumpkin pie spice
1 cup sugar
1½ cups flour
¾ cup walnuts, chopped

Combine eggs, butter, pumpkin, soda, salt, cinnamon, pumpkin pie spice, sugar, and flour. Mix well, fold in walnuts, and pour in prepared loaf pan. Bake at 375 degrees for 45 to 50 minutes.

—ShadowCat

20 Saturday

3rd ♓
Color: Blue

Execution of Lancashire Witches, 1612
Birthday of H. P. Lovecraft, horror
writer and alleged magician, 1890
Birthday of Ann Moura, author and Witch

21 Sunday

3rd ♓
☽ v/c 5:45 am
☽ enters ♈ 7:01 pm
Color: Yellow

When fishing, throw back the first fish you catch as
payment to Neptune; then you will catch many more

August

22 Monday

3rd ♈
☉ enters ♍ 8:45 pm
Color: Ivory

Sun enters Virgo
Pope John XXII orders the
Inquisition at Carcassonne to seize
the property of Witches, sorcerers, and
those who make wax images, 1320

23 Tuesday

3rd ♈
☽ v/c 7:46 am
☽ enters ♉ 9:58 pm
Color: Scarlet

*The flowering vine jasmine corresponds to the Moon
and is used to promote sensuality and loving enchantments*

24 Wednesday

3rd ♉
Color: White

25 Thursday

3rd ♉
☽ v/c 2:14 am
Color: Crimson

☽ Friday

3rd ♉
☽ enters ♊ 4:43 am
4th Quarter 11:18 am
Color: Rose

To bring rain, burn fern leaves outside

Set in Eastern Daylight Time (EDT)

27 Saturday
4th ♊
☽ v/c 10:49 pm
Color: Brown

28 Sunday
4th ♊
☽ enters ♋ 2:57 pm
Color: Gold

August/September

29 Monday
4th ♋
Color: Gray

Election of Pope Innocent VIII, who issued
bull *Summis Desiderantes Affectibus*, 1484

30 Tuesday
4th ♋
☽ v/c 3:22 am
Color: Maroon

31 Wednesday
4th ♋
☽ enters ♌ 3:14 am
Color: Brown

Birthday of Raymond Buckland,
who, along with his wife Rosemary,
is generally credited with bringing
Gardnerian Wicca to the United States

1 Thursday
4th ♌
Color: White

2 Friday
4th ♌
♇ D 6:52 am
☽ v/c 7:44 am
☽ enters ♍ 3:56 pm
Color: Pink

Celtic Tree Month of Vine begins
Birthday of Reverend Paul
Beyerl, Wiccan author

An Exploration of Ethics

Pins and needles, spools and threads
Craft our lives from scraps and shreds.
All we make is all we see
Coming back to us, times three.

Milk and cookies, bread and beer
Teach the taste of hope and fear.
Swallow lies, and there's the fee
Coming back to us, times three.

Bags and bottles, cups and cans
Sort the contents of our spans.
What we choose may set us free
Coming back to us, times three.

—Elizabeth Barrette

☽ Saturday

4th ♍
New Moon 2:45 pm
Color: Black

4 Sunday

1st ♍
☽ v/c 11:40 am
☿ enters ♍ 1:52 pm
Color: Orange

*Red begonias or scarlet geraniums planted in window
boxes bestow protection on the home and all who live there*

September

5 Monday

1st ♍

☽ enters ♎ 3:52 am

Color: Lavender

Labor Day

6 Tuesday

1st ♎

Color: Red

Chrysanthemums are magical fall flowers;
their spicy scent bestows protection and their
jewel-bright colors are uplifting and cheerful

7 Wednesday

1st ♎

☽ v/c 4:33 am

☽ enters ♏ 2:10 pm

Color: Yellow

8 Thursday

1st ♏

Color: Purple

Founding of the Theosophical
Society by H. P. Blavatsky, Henry
Steele Olcott, and others, 1875

9 Friday

1st ♏

☽ v/c 3:31 am

☽ enters ♐ 10:03 pm

Color: Coral

Set in Eastern Daylight Time (EDT)

10 Saturday

1st ♐
Color: Brown

Birthday of Carl Llewellyn
Weschcke, owner and president
of Llewellyn Worldwide

◖ Sunday

1st ♐
2nd Quarter 7:37 am
♀ enters ♏ 12:14 pm
☽ v/c 12:52 pm
Color: Yellow

Birthday of Silver RavenWolf,
Wiccan author

September

12 Monday
2nd ♐
☽ enters ♑ 2:56 am
Color: Gray

13 Tuesday
2nd ♑
☽ v/c 2:22 pm
Color: Black

*Keep an acorn on the windowsill or use it as a windowshade
pull; it grants protection, especially from lightning strikes*

14 Wednesday
2nd ♑
☽ enters ♒ 5:02 am
Color: White

Phillip IV of France draws up
the order for the arrest of
the French Templars, 1306

Birthday of Henry Cornelius Agrippa,
scholar and magician, 1486

15 Thursday
2nd ♒
☽ v/c 4:23 pm
Color: Turquoise

16 Friday
2nd ♒
☽ enters ♓ 5:24 am
Color: Rose

*Agates are a great all-purpose stone; match up
the color of the agate to your magical intention*

Set in Eastern Daylight Time (EDT)

September

A fter the Moon makes its last major aspect with another planet before moving into a new sign, it is "void-of-course." Many Witches will not begin a new magical effort or study until this time (ranging from a few minutes to all day) has passed.

Instead of moaning about having to put off your new spell, think of the void-of-course Moon as taking her time of rest. Thank her during this time for all her help and teaching. Light a candle in her honor. Ask nothing of her—offer only your gratitude.

> *Virgin, mother, crone she may be,*
> *Her silver light still shines within me.*
> *I bless you for the gift of light,*
> *I bless the dawn and the blue twilight.*
> *Hidden, obscure, and I can't always see you,*
> *But I know you are there, shining through.*
> *Rest now, dear Goddess, in slumber keep,*
> *Your own sweet dreams enhance your sleep.*

—Edain McCoy

☺ Saturday

2nd ♓
Full Moon 10:01 pm
☽ v/c 10:01 pm
Color: Blue

Harvest Moon
Bewitched debuts on ABC-TV, 1964

---

18 Sunday

3rd ♓
☽ enters ♈ 5:43 am
Color: Gold

---

19 Monday
3rd ♈
♀ enters ♏ 2:10 am
☽ v/c 6:36 pm
Color: White

*Hang a small set of wind chimes indoors; their happy sound
dispels any negative vibrations that may be lurking about*

20 Tuesday
3rd ♈
☽ enters ♉ 7:47 am
☿ enters ♎ 12:40 pm
Color: Maroon

21 Wednesday
3rd ♉
Color: Topaz

*Never use iron to harvest plants used for
magic, as its touch dispels their power*

22 Thursday
3rd ♉
☽ v/c 12:41 pm
☽ enters ♊ 1:07 pm
☉ enters ♎ 6:23 pm
Color: Green

Mabon/Fall Equinox
Sun enters Libra

23 Friday
3rd ♊
♃ enters ♐ 10:19 pm
Color: Purple

Mabon

At the Autumnal Equinox, Persephone descends beneath the Earth to become the Queen of the Underworld until spring. To reenact this journey, you need to have access to a set of stairs, preferably to a basement, that you can have exclusive use of for the ritual. Choose seven pieces of clothing and jewelry that can symbolize seven gates to the underworld. We use shoes, sash or cords, robe, ring, athame, necklace, and crown. Take off all other clothing and put on those seven items.

Start at the top of the stairs and say, "I will journey with you, Great Queen, to your home in the underworld," Take two steps down, remove your shoes, and say, "I pass the first gate, and lay down my shoes." Take two more steps down, remove your sash, and say, "I pass the second gate, and lay down my sash." Proceed down the steps until you come to the bottom. There, take up a dish with pomegranate seeds, pomegranate wine, or other dark red wine. Meditate on the underworld, the place of death and knowledge. Eat the seeds or drink the wine. Then return up the stairs, gathering what you have discarded as you go, but not looking behind you.

—Magenta Griffith

24 Saturday

3rd ♊
☽ v/c 8:57 am
☽ enters ♋ 10:10 pm
Color: Indigo

○ Sunday

3rd ♋
4th Quarter 2:41 am
Color: Amber

Senate passes an amendment (705)
attached by Senator Jesse Helms to House
Resolution 3036 (1986 budget bill),
denying tax-exempt status to any organization
that espouses satanism or witchcraft, 1985

26 Monday
4th ♋
☽ v/c 9:24 pm
Color: Ivory

Joan Wiliford hanged at Faversham,
England, 1645; she testified that
the Devil came to her in the form of a
black dog that she called "Bunnie"

27 Tuesday
4th ♋
☽ enters ♌ 10:03 am
Color: White

28 Wednesday
4th ♌
Color: Brown

29 Thursday
4th ♌
☽ v/c 11:12 am
☽ enters ♍ 10:44 pm
Color: Crimson

*Plant your spring bulbs in the waning
Moon of September or October for best results*

30 Friday
4th ♍
Color: White

Celtic Tree Month of Ivy begins

Set in Eastern Daylight Time (EDT)

Rutabaga Delight

1 rutabaga, peeled and sliced into
   thin pieces
5 medium russet potatoes, peeled
   and cut into chunks
½ stick butter
Salt and pepper to taste
½ cup milk (more or less)

Bring a large pot of water to boil and add rutabaga. Cook for 20 minutes, then add potatoes. Cook until both vegetables are soft. Drain water. Add butter and begin mashing. Add salt and fresh ground pepper to taste. Add milk and mash to desired consistency. Serve with roast beef and a garden salad.

—ShadowCat

1 Saturday
4th ♍
♂ ℞ 6:04 pm
☽ v/c 9:22 pm
Color: Gray

Birthday of Isaac Bonewitz,
Druid, magician, and Witch

Birthday of Annie Besant,
Theosophical Society president, 1847

2 Sunday
4th ♍
☽ enters ♎ 10:24 am
Color: Yellow

Birthday of Timothy Roderick,
Wiccan author

☽ Monday
4th ♎︎
New Moon 6:28 am
Color: White

Solar eclipse 6:33 am, 10° ♎︎ 19'

4 Tuesday
1st ♎︎
☽ v/c 11:15 am
☽ enters ♏︎ 8:03 pm
Color: Red

Rosh Hashanah
Ramadan begins
President Reagan signs JR 165 making
1983 "The Year of the Bible" (public law
#9728Q); the law states that the Bible is
the word of God and urges a return to
"traditional" Christian values, 1982

5 Wednesday
1st ♏︎
⚷ D 1:32 am
Color: Topaz

*Painting the ceiling of your porch sky blue
frightens away ghosts and wandering spirits; in the old
South this special color was called "haint blue"*

6 Thursday
1st ♏︎
Color: Purple

7 Friday
1st ♏︎
☽ v/c 1:51 am
☽ enters ♐︎ 3:28 am
♀ enters ♐︎ 9:00 pm
Color: Pink

Birthday of Arnold Crowther, stage
magician and Gardnerian Witch, 1909

8 Saturday

1st ♐

☿ enters ♏ 1:15 pm

Color: Black

Sweet, spicy sandalwood oil lessens
inhibitions and frees the imagination

9 Sunday

1st ♐

☽ v/c 2:20 am

☽ enters ♑ 8:43 am

Color: Orange

October

◐ Monday
1st ♑
2nd Quarter 3:01 pm
Color: Lavender

Columbus Day (observed)

11 Tuesday
2nd ♑
☽ v/c 6:42 am
☽ enters ♒ 12:05 pm
Color: White

12 Wednesday
2nd ♒
Color: Yellow

Birthday of Aleister Crowley, 1875

13 Thursday
2nd ♒
☽ v/c 9:34 am
☽ enters ♓ 2:05 pm
Color: Turquoise

Yom Kippur
Jacques de Molay and other
French Templars arrested by
order of King Phillip IV, 1306

14 Friday
2nd ♓
Color: Rose

Tuck a holey stone under your front porch
to ward the house and protect the family

Set in Eastern Daylight Time (EDT)

Lunar Eclipse

The second face of the lunar eclipse can assist your spirit to move out of the shadows that hide the best in you, igniting an epiphany of spirit which is part of your wholeness.

Lie down under the light of the Full Moon (indoors or out) and close your eyes. Visualize yourself glowing with a warm silver light that illuminates your soul. Focus on the light as it wanes. Shadows begins to obscure the clarity with which you perceive yourself. Allow the darkness to remind you that imperfection is part of the whole and that wisdom is attained by first passing through the darkness.

Continue to lie still as the Moon's light emerges from shadow and begins to illuminate the darkened Earth again. Connect with the light by visualizing yourself filling with the universal light of wisdom. You may need to undergo many such rituals to fully integrate your dark and light sides, learning the enlightenment that you can receive only by coming full circle from light to darkness to the rebirth into light.

—Edain McCoy

15 Saturday
2nd ♓
☽ v/c 2:55 am
☽ enters ♈ 3:39 pm
Color: Indigo

This fall, pick up a fallen acorn and slip it into your pocket; acorns promote fertility and symbolize the God

16 Sunday
2nd ♈
Color: Amber

October

☺ Monday

2nd ♈

Full Moon 8:14 am

☽ v/c 2:58 pm

☽ enters ♉ 6:04 pm

Color: Ivory

Blood Moon

Lunar eclipse 8:04 am, 24° ♈ 13'

18 Tuesday

3rd ♉

Color: Gray

Sukkot begins

Birthday of Nicholas Culpepper,
astrologer and herbalist, 1616

19 Wednesday

3rd ♉

☽ v/c 6:50 am

☽ enters ♊ 10:44 pm

Color: Brown

20 Thursday

3rd ♊

Color: Green

Birthday of Selena Fox, Circle Sanctuary

21 Friday

3rd ♊

Color: White

October

Samhain is a time for us to remember those who have passed before, and to be their link to those who come after. On October 17, the Full Moon will shed its silver glow through our night skies. But the very next day the Moon begins to wane again, making the night skies darker until it vanishes from sight on October 31.

Each night from October 17 to Samhain Eve, take some time to look at the Moon and feel her taking you closer to the veil that opens between our worlds on Samhain.

> Shrinking, fading, mother Moon,
> Your crone-age time is coming soon;
> Your wrinkled face and cloak of winter,
> We invite you to share our ritual dinner.
> Blessed Crone, the centuries have passed,
> Yet through each winter harsh you last.
> Find room to shelter us, Crone and mother,
> And remind us to share our blessings with others.

—Edain McCoy

---

22 Saturday

3rd ♊
☽ v/c 5:07 am
☽ enters ♋ 6:41 am
Color: Blue

Knots can trap malignant spirits; a knotted fringe makes the perfect finishing touch on an altar cloth

---

23 Sunday

3rd ♋
☉ enters ♏ 3:42 am
Color: Gold

Sun enters Scorpio

October

◑ Monday
3rd ♋
☽ v/c 5:16 pm
☽ enters ♌ 5:48 pm
4th Quarter 9:17 pm
Color: Silver

Sukkot ends

25 Tuesday
4th ♌
♃ enters ♏ 10:52 pm
Color: Scarlet

Jacques de Molay first interrogated
after Templar arrest, 1306

26 Wednesday
4th ♌
♆ D 7:24 pm
☽ v/c 10:23 pm
Color: White

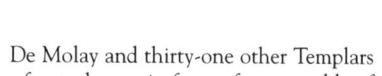

De Molay and thirty-one other Templars
confess to heresy in front of an assembly of
clergy; all later recant their confessions, 1306
Sybil Leek dies of cancer, 1982

27 Thursday
4th ♌
☽ enters ♍ 6:28 am
Color: Purple

Circle Sanctuary founded, 1974

28 Friday
4th ♍
Color: Coral

Celtic Tree Month of Reed begins

Samhain

Samhain means "summer's end" in Gaelic, and for many Witches it is also the New Year. Traditionally, tonight is the time when the veil between the worlds is thinnest. This means that one can more easily be in touch with entities from other planes—from ghosts to gods. It also means that divination is very effective on this night.

If you have no other plans, take out a tarot deck and ask the question, "What will my life be like in the coming year?" Or, you and a friend could try the Ouija board. Sit facing each other in straight-backed chairs. Balance the board on both your knees. Each of you puts one hand on the planchette. After a while, it will begin to move of its own accord. Note the letters it moves to, and see what it spells out. You may need to keep at it for a while; it's usually nonsense at first. If you don't have a Ouija board, you can improvise one by writing the letters of the alphabet and the numbers 1 through 0 out on separate pieces of paper (3 x 5 cards cut in half work well). Arrange these in a circle on a table. Turn a small glass upside down and use it as you would the planchette.

—Magenta Griffith

---

29 Saturday

4th ♍
☽ v/c 5:06 pm
☽ enters ♎ 6:15 pm
Color: Black

MacGregor Mathers issues manifesto calling himself supreme leader of the Golden Dawn; all members had to sign an oath of fealty to him, 1896

Birthday of Frater Zarathustra, who founded the Temple of Truth in 1972

---

30 Sunday

4th ♎
☿ enters ♐ 4:02 am
Color: Orange

Daylight Saving Time ends at 2 am

House-Senate conferees drop the Senate provision barring the IRS from granting tax-exempt status to groups that promote satanism or witchcraft, 1985

PACT (Pagan Awareness Coalition for Teens) established in Omaha, Nebraska, 2001

---

31 Monday

4th ♎︎
☽ v/c 6:17 pm
Color: Lavender

Samhain/Halloween
Martin Luther nails his ninety-five theses
to the door of Wittenburg Castle Church,
igniting the Protestant revolution, 1517
Covenant of the Goddess founded, 1975

☽ Tuesday

4th ♎︎
☽ enters ♏︎ 2:29 am
✳ ℞ 4:45 pm
New Moon 8:25 pm
Color: Gray

All Saints' Day
Aquarian Tabernacle Church established
in the United States, 1979

2 Wednesday

1st ♏︎
☽ v/c 9:05 am
Color: Yellow

Circle Sanctuary purchases land
for nature preserve, 1983

3 Thursday

1st ♏︎
☽ enters ♐︎ 8:55 am
Color: Turquoise

Ramadan ends

4 Friday

1st ♐︎
Color: White

November

English-speaking North Americans seem to have adopted the Mexican folk festival *Dia de los Muertos*, or Day of the Dead, which falls on November 2—the same day as the New Moon.

To connect with the atmosphere of the day, hang small skeletons called *calaveras* on bushes and trees. Hang crêpe paper all over your home—and your family cemetery—and be sure to display all those family photos of ancestors. Collect the photos on an altar to honor your ancestors and let them know they are welcome.

> *Between our worlds the veil is thin,*
> *A chance to invite our family in.*
> *From their world to ours, we make the call,*
> *We welcome our ancestors, welcome all.*

Leave an offering of food for your night visitors, and leave a light to illuminate their path.

—Edain McCoy

---

5 Saturday
1st ♐
☽ v/c 12:58 am
♀ enters ♑ 3:10 am
☽ enters ♑ 1:17 pm
Color: Blue

---

6 Sunday
1st ♑
☽ v/c 3:18 pm
Color: Amber

Arrange apples, ornamental corn, and
mini-pumpkins into a basket; enchant them for
wisdom, prosperity, and a happy harvest season

November

7 Monday

1st ♑
☽ enters ♒ 4:31 pm
Color: Lavender

Samhain crossquarter day
(Sun reaches 15° Scorpio)

◑ Tuesday

1st ♒
2nd Quarter 8:57 pm
Color: White

Election Day (general)

Sentencing of Witches in
Basque Zugarramurdi trial, 1610

Marriage of Patricia and Arnold Crowther
officiated by Gerald Gardner, 1960

9 Wednesday

2nd ♒
☽ v/c 7:31 am
☽ enters ♓ 7:22 pm
Color: Brown

Patricia and Arnold Crowther
married in civil ceremony, 1960

10 Thursday

2nd ♓
Color: Purple

11 Friday

2nd ♓
☽ v/c 10:33 am
☽ enters ♈ 10:22 pm
Color: Coral

Veterans Day

Set in Eastern Standard Time (EST)

The Legacy of Loss

Loss cuts us loose to begin again.
The shears snip through the cord,
And the Crone sets the pieces aside.
Some knots need a sharp answer.

The shears snip through the cord
After we tangle ourselves up
In knots that need a sharp answer.
She does not condemn for what we do.

After we tangle ourselves up
And the Crone sets the pieces aside,
She does not condemn for what we do.
Loss cuts us loose to begin again.

—Elizabeth Barrette

12 Saturday
2nd ♈
Color: Indigo

Petrified wood grants longevity and aids in exploring past lives

13 Sunday
2nd ♈
☽ v/c 2:07 pm
Color: Orange

November

14 Monday

2nd ♈
☿ ℞ 12:42 am
☽ enters ♉ 2:02 am
Color: Silver

*Carry a small golden-striped tiger's-eye in
your pocket for success and protection*

☺ Tuesday

2nd ♉
♅ D 7:07 pm
Full Moon 7:58 pm
☽ v/c 7:58 pm
Color: Black

*Mourning Moon
Aquarian Tabernacle Church
established in Canada, 1993*

16 Wednesday

3rd ♉
☽ enters ♊ 7:10 am
Color: White

17 Thursday

3rd ♊
Color: Crimson

*Birthday of Israel Regardie, occultist
and member of the OTO, 1907*

18 Friday

3rd ♊
☽ v/c 2:02 am
☽ enters ♋ 2:42 pm
♇ ℞ 6:41 pm
Color: Pink

*Aleister Crowley initiated into the
Golden Dawn as Frater Perdurabo, 1898*

Harvest Stew

1 lb. beef stew meat cut in
   1-inch cubes
½ cup flour
2 tbs. lard
4 medium russet potatoes, un-
   peeled, cut into chunks
1 small bag baby carrots
1 large yellow onion, chopped
1 cup rutabaga, chopped
1 cup frozen peas
1 clove garlic, minced
1 stalk celery, chopped
1 cup beef broth
1 pkg. dry onion soup mix
1 can condensed mushroom soup

Dredge beef in flour. Heat skillet, then add lard. Brown beef on all sides. Place all vegetables in crockpot. Place beef on top of vegetables. Add broth, onion soup mix, and condensed mushroom soup. Cover crockpot and set on low for 10 to 12 hours or on high for 4 to 5 hours. Do not open the crockpot during cooking time. Season with salt and pepper as individual taste requires. Serve with a hearty, crusty bread and garden salad.

—ShadowCat

19 Saturday

3rd ♋
Color: Gray

Birthday of Theodore
Parker Mills, Wiccan elder, 1924

20 Sunday

3rd ♋
☽ v/c 11:03 pm
Color: Yellow

Church of All Worlds
incorporates in Australia, 1992

November

21 Monday

3rd ♋
☽ enters ♌ 1:10 am
Color: Ivory

22 Tuesday

3rd ♌
☉ enters ♐ 12:15 am
♄ ℞ 4:01 am
Color: Maroon

Sun enters Sagittarius

◯ Wednesday

3rd ♌
☽ v/c 12:25 am
☽ enters ♍ 1:41 pm
4th Quarter 5:11 pm
Color: Topaz

Birthday of Lady Tamara Von Forslun,
founder of the Church of Wicca and the
Aquarian Tabernacle Church in Australia

24 Thursday
4th ♍
Color: Green

Thanksgiving Day

25 Friday
4th ♍
☽ v/c 1:10 pm
Color: Rose

Celtic Tree Month of Elder begins
Dr. John Dee notes Edward
Kelly's death in his diary, 1595

Set in Eastern Standard Time (EST)

On the Solitary Trail

I am a cat made of shadows and snow,
As solitary as the moon supreme.
I make my own trail wherever I go.

Ice in the starlight and frost on the floe,
As subtle as smoke and as smooth as cream,
I am a cat made of shadows and snow.

Oath or allegiance to none do I owe;
I never belonged to anyone's team.
I make my own trail wherever I go.

I am the strength of the north winds that blow,
Efficient and swift, secure in esteem.
I am a cat made of shadows and snow.

Shaman and shapeshifter whisper below.
Two feet in this world, and two in a dream,
I make my own trail wherever I go.

Here is my circle, these trees bowing low.
Here is my magic, this breathing of steam.
I am a cat made of shadows and snow;
I make my own trail wherever I go.

—Elizabeth Barrette

---

26 Saturday
4th ♍
☽ enters ♎ 1:58 am
☿ enters ♏ 6:53 am
Color: Black

---

27 Sunday
4th ♎
♀ enters ♐ 9:32 am
☽ v/c 11:38 pm
Color: Gold

Essential oil of gardenia promotes trust, love, and spirituality

---

28 Monday
4th ♎︎
☽ enters ♏︎ 11:33 am
Color: Gray

When you get a new coat, put a coin
in the right-hand pocket for good luck

29 Tuesday
4th ♏︎
Color: Red

30 Wednesday
4th ♏︎
☽ v/c 10:16 am
☽ enters ♐︎ 5:32 pm
Color: Brown

Birthday of Oberon Zell,
Church of All Worlds
Father Urbain Grandier imprisoned in
France for bewitching nuns, 1633

☽ Thursday
4th ♐︎
New Moon 10:01 am
Color: Purple

Birthday of Anodea Judith,
president, Church of All Worlds

2 Friday
1st ♐︎
☽ v/c 10:17 am
☽ enters ♑︎ 8:42 pm
Color: Coral

3 Saturday

1st ♑
☿ D 9:22 pm
Color: Brown

*Decorate your Yule wreaths with the magical duo of holly
and ivy; this promotes protection, fidelity, and good luck*

4 Sunday

1st ♑
☽ v/c 1:56 pm
☽ enters ♒ 10:36 pm
Color: Yellow

December

5 Monday

1st ≈
♅ enters ≈ 8:10 pm
Color: Silver

Pope Innocent VIII reverses the
Canon Episcopi by issuing the bull
Summis Desiderantes Affectibus, removing
obstacles to Inquisitors, 1484
Death of Aleister Crowley, 1947

6 Tuesday

1st ≈
☽ v/c 4:58 pm
Color: Black

Death of Jacob Sprenger, coauthor
of the *Malleus Maleficarum*, 1495
Birthday of Dion Fortune, member
of the Golden Dawn, 1890

7 Wednesday

1st ≈
☽ enters ♓ 12:44 am
Color: White

*Set out a few clusters of quartz crystals in the main room
of your house; they keep the family on a positive track*

○ Thursday

1st ♓
2nd Quarter 4:36 am
☽ v/c 11:16 pm
Color: Turquoise

9 Friday

2nd ♓
☽ enters ♈ 4:02 am
♂ D 11:03 pm
Color: White

*Wintergreen oil has a refreshing,
energizing effect that also conveys wisdom*

Set in Eastern Standard Time (EST)

Mother's Yule Log

1 lb. graham crackers, crushed
1 lb. walnuts, chopped
1 lb. miniature marshmallows
1 lb. dates, chopped
½ pint heavy cream
whipped cream

Mix all ingredients together, reserving some of the graham crackers. Roll into a loaf, then cover with reserved graham crackers and wrap in waxed paper and refrigerate. Chill, slice, and serve with whipped cream.

—ShadowCat

10 Saturday
2nd ♈
Color: Gray

11 Sunday

2nd ♈
☽ v/c 5:50 am
♀ enters ♑ 8:41 am
☽ enters ♉ 8:46 am
Color: Orange

12 Monday

2nd ♉
☿ enters ♐ 4:19 pm
Color: Lavender

Decorate the Yule log with both holly (masculine) and ivy
(feminine)—to naturally represent the God and the Goddess

13 Tuesday

2nd ♉
☽ v/c 1:46 pm
☽ enters ♊ 2:59 pm
Color: Maroon

First papal bull against black magic
issued by Alexander IV, 1258

14 Wednesday
2nd ♊
Color: Brown

☺ Thursday
2nd ♊
♀ enters ≈ 10:57 am
Full Moon 11:16 am
☽ v/c 12:11 pm
☽ enters ♋ 11:01 pm
Color: Green

Long Nights Moon

16 Friday

3rd ♋
☽ v/c 7:33 pm
Color: Pink

December

December is full of holidays and celebrations honoring the return of the Sun to the Earth. The solstice celebration that dominates our culture today is Christmas. It's a Christian celebration of a God reborn, yet its energy, decor, and customs are pure Pagan.

The virgin waxing crescent of the Moon on the 23rd makes a perfect link between the solstice of the 21st and the Christmas celebration on the 25th. In many families both holidays are celebrated, and the waxing crescent allows us all to "meet in the middle" to honor a celestial body as old as the Earth itself.

If possible, gather outside. If that's not practical, use your own living room with all the lighted symbols of the season around you. Hold hands and appoint a spokesperson.

> *Hanukkah, Midwinter, Kwanzaa, Yule,*
> *Christmas, Boxing Day, and St. Stephen's too.*
> *Bless all those who come together in peace,*
> *Creator, we ask your blessing on each.*

—Edain McCoy

17 Saturday
3rd ♋
Color: Blue

Turquoise beads or rings can be worn to promote good health and prosperity, and to prevent accidents

18 Sunday
3rd ♋
☽ enters ♌ 9:18 am
Color: Amber

19 Monday
3rd ♌
Color: Gray

*Wear malachite touching your skin if you want to
expand your heart's ability to love and to attract a lover*

20 Tuesday
3rd ♌
☽ v/c 8:09 pm
☽ enters ♍ 9:39 pm
Color: Red

21 Wednesday
3rd ♍
☉ enters ♑ 1:35 pm
Color: Yellow

Yule/Winter Solstice
Sun enters Capricorn

22 Thursday
3rd ♍
☽ v/c 11:30 pm
Color: Crimson

Janet and Stewart Farrar begin
their first coven together, 1970

☾ Friday
3rd ♍
☽ enters ♎ 10:26 am
4th Quarter 2:36 pm
Color: Coral

Yule

Gather with friends at sunrise, or as soon after as possible, on the Winter Solstice. Meditate on the idea that this is the darkest time of the year, but that the light will return. As it is in the circle of the year, so may it be in the world: that as the light grows, illumination and warmth extend throughout the globe. Concentrate on the idea of peace, understanding, and harmony between all peoples spreading as the light of the Sun spreads. Resolve to be  a more peaceful person in the coming year, and think of ways you could promote understanding. Feel in your heart of hearts that peace is not only possible but inevitable, that the time of war is over, that the human race is evolving past such foolish pursuits. Then sing a song of peace, like "Imagine" or "Give Peace a Chance" by John Lennon; "Universal Soldier" by Donovan; or "Last Night I Had the Strangest Dream," which has been recorded by Joan Baez, the Weavers, and Pete Seeger, among others. If you are alone and don't wish to sing, play a peaceful selection of music—either folk songs or music like Pachebel's *Canon* or Debussy's *La Mer*—while concentrating on the same ideas.

—Magenta Griffith

24 Saturday

4th ♎
♀ ℞ 4:36 am
Color: Indigo

Christmas Eve
Celtic Tree Month of Birch begins

25 Sunday

4th ♎
☽ v/c 10:53 am
☽ enters ♏ 9:04 pm
Color: Gold

Christmas Day
Feast of Frau Holle, Germanic weather goddess who was believed to travel through the world to watch people's deeds; she blessed the good and punished the bad

December/January

26 Monday
4th ♏
Color: Ivory

Kwanzaa begins

Hanukkah begins

Dr. Fian arraigned for twenty counts
of witchcraft and treason, 1590

27 Tuesday
4th ♏
☽ v/c 2:26 am
Color: Scarlet

Birthday of Gerina Dunwich,
Wiccan author

28 Wednesday
4th ♏
☽ enters ♐ 3:43 am
Color: Topaz

29 Thursday
4th ♐
☽ v/c 10:01 pm
Color: White

*Wearing amethyst jewelry helps keep you
calm and centered; it's a great de-stressing stone*

 Friday
4th ♐
☽ enters ♑ 6:35 am
New Moon 10:12 pm
Color: Purple

Set in Eastern Standard Time (EST)

31 Saturday

1st ♑
☽ v/c 4:09 am
Color: Black

New Year's Eve
Castle of Countess Bathory of Hungary
raided, 1610; accused of practicing black
magic, she murdered scores of the local
townsfolk; she was walled up in a room in
her castle, where she later died

1 Sunday

1st ♑
☽ enters ♒ 7:14 am
♀ enters ♑ 3:18 pm
Color: Yellow

Kwanzaa ends
New Year's Day

About the Authors

ELIZABETH BARRETTE serves as the managing editor of *PanGaia* and assistant editor of *SageWoman*. She has been involved with the Pagan community for more than fifteen years, and in 2003 earned ordination as a priestess through Sanctuary of the Silver Moon. She also won the *Sol Magazine* competition for Poet Laureate 2003. Her other writing fields include speculative fiction and gender studies. She lives in central Illinois and enjoys herbal landscaping and gardening for wildlife.

ELLEN DUGAN, the "Garden Witch," is a psychic-clairvoyant and has been a practicing Witch for over eighteen years. Ellen is a master gardener and teaches classes on flower folklore and gardening at a community college. She is the author of the Llewellyn books *Garden Witchery*; *Elements of Witchcraft*; *Natural Magick for Teens*; and *Seven Days of Magick*. Ellen and her family live in Missouri.

GERINA DUNWICH, born under the sign of Capricorn with an Aries rising, is a priestess of the old religion, astrologer, founder of the Pagan Poets Society, and author of two dozen books on Wicca, spellcasting, and the occult. She currently resides in southern California.

EMELY FLAK has been a practicing solitary Witch for ten years. She is a freelance writer based in Daylesford, Australia, and is also employed as a learning and development professional. Much of her work is dedicated to embracing the ancient wisdom of Wicca for the personal empowerment of women in the competitive work environment.

MAGENTA GRIFFITH has been a Witch for over twenty-five years and a high priestess for over thirteen years, and is a founding member of the coven Prodea, which has been together since 1980. She presents workshops and classes around the Midwest and is a cofounder of the New Alexandria Library in Minneapolis, which is a Pagan and magical resource center.

JAMES KAMBOS is a writer and folk artist. He holds a degree in history and has had a lifelong interest in folk magic. He has written numerous articles on the folk magic traditions of Greece, the Near East, and the Appalachian region of the United States. When not writing and painting from his home in Appalachia, he enjoys working in his herb garden.

EDAIN MCCOY has practiced Witchcraft for more than twenty years and has studied many magical traditions, including Wiccan, Judaic, Celtic, Appalachian, and Curanderismo traditions. She is listed in the reference books *Who's Who in America* and *Contemporary Authors*. When the economy began to slow in 2001, Edain made the difficult decision to leave her career as a stockbroker in order to write full time. She is the author of nineteen Llewellyn books, including *A Witch's Guide to Faery Folk, The Sabbats, Celtic Myth and Magick, The Witches' Coven, Making Magic, Celtic Women's Spirituality, Astral Projection for Beginners, Enchantments, Ostara, Spellworking for Covens, Advanced Witchcraft,* and *If You Want to Be a Witch*.

SHADOWCAT is a Witch in the American Celtic Tradition of Lady Sheba, but prefers solitary work. She spends her days acquiring new manuscripts for Llewellyn Publications, and her free time fussing around her house, mostly in the kitchen. Born with epicurean tastes, she says life is too short to eat bad food. She considers her bread maker, her stand mixer, and her food processor her "power tools." ShadowCat shares her home with four feline companions who have their own fine china for dining on Fancy Feast.

JULIANNA YAU is a freelance writer and artist residing in Canada. She has several articles published in Llewellyn's annuals.

Appendix

Daily Magical Influences

Each day is ruled by a planet with specific magical influences.
Monday (Moon): peace, healing, caring, psychic awareness
Tuesday (Mars): passion, courage, aggression, protection
Wednesday (Mercury): study, travel, divination, wisdom
Thursday (Jupiter): expansion, money, prosperity, generosity
Friday (Venus): love, friendship, reconciliation, beauty
Saturday (Saturn): longevity, endings, homes
Sunday (Sun): healing, spirituality, success, strength, protection

Color Correspondences

Colors are associated with each day, according to planetary influence.
Monday: gray, lavender, white, silver, ivory
Tuesday: red, white, black, gray, maroon, scarlet
Wednesday: yellow, brown, white, topaz
Thursday: green, turquoise, white, purple, crimson
Friday: white, pink, rose, purple, coral
Saturday: brown, gray, blue, indigo, black
Sunday: yellow, orange, gold, amber

Lunar Phases

Waxing, from New Moon to Full Moon, is the ideal time to do magic to draw things to you.

Waning, from Full Moon to New Moon, is a time for study, meditation, and magical work designed to banish harmful energies.

The Moon's Sign

The Moon continuously moves through each sign of the zodiac, from Aries to Pisces, staying about two and a half days in each sign. The Moon influences the sign it inhabits, creating different energies that affect our day-to-day lives.

Aries: Good for starting things. Things occur rapidly, but quickly pass. People tend to be argumentative and assertive.

Taurus: Things begun now last longest, tend to increase in value, and become hard to change. Brings out an appreciation for beauty and sensory experience.

Gemini: Things begun now are easily changed by outside influence. Time for shortcuts, communication, games, and fun.

Cancer: Stimulates emotional rapport between people. Supports growth and nurturing. Tend to domestic concerns.

Leo: Draws emphasis to the self, to central ideas or institutions, away from connections with others and emotional needs.

Virgo: Favors accomplishment of details and commands from higher up. Focus on health, hygiene, and daily schedules.

Libra: Favors cooperation, compromise, social activities, balance, friendship, and partnership.

Scorpio: Increases awareness of psychic power. Precipitates psychic crises and ends connections thoroughly. People tend to brood and become secretive.

Sagittarius: Encourages confidence and flights of imagination. This is an adventurous, philosophical, and athletic Moon sign. Favors expansion and growth.

Capricorn: Develops strong structure. Focus on traditions, responsibilities, and obligations. A good time to set boundaries and rules.

Aquarius: Rebellious energy. Time to break habits and make abrupt change. Personal freedom and individuality is the focus.

Pisces: The focus is on dreaming, nostalgia, intuition, and psychic impressions. A good time for spiritual or philanthropic activities.

2005 Eclipses

April 8, 4:37 pm; Solar eclipse 19° ♈ 06'
April 24, 5:56 am; Lunar eclipse 4° ♏ 20'
October 3, 6:33 am; Solar eclipse 10° ♎ 19'
October 17, 8:04 am; Lunar eclipse 24° ♈ 13'

2005 Full Moons

Cold Moon: January 25, 5:32 am
Quickening Moon: February 23, 11:54 pm
Storm Moon: March 25, 3:58 pm
Wind Moon: April 24, 6:06 am
Flower Moon: May 23, 4:18 pm
Strong Sun Moon: June 22, 12:14 am
Blessing Moon: July 21, 7:00 am
Corn Moon: August 19, 1:53 pm
Harvest Moon: September 17, 10:01 pm
Blood Moon: October 17, 8:14 am
Mourning Moon: November 15, 7:58 pm
Long Nights Moon: December 15, 11:16 am

Planetary Retrogrades in 2005

Saturn	℞	11/08/04	1:54 am	—	Direct	03/21/05	9:54 pm
Jupiter	℞	02/01/05	9:26 pm	—	Direct	06/05/05	3:20 am
Mercury	℞	03/19/05	7:13 pm	—	Direct	04/12/05	3:45 am
Pluto	℞	03/26/05	9:29 pm	—	Direct	09/02/05	6:52 am
Neptune	℞	05/19/05	7:36 pm	—	Direct	10/26/05	7:24 pm
Uranus	℞	06/14/05	6:38 pm	—	Direct	11/15/05	7:07 pm
Mercury	℞	07/22/05	10:59 pm	—	Direct	08/15/05	11:49 pm
Mars	℞	10/01/05	6:04 pm	—	Direct	12/09/05	11:03 pm
Mercury	℞	11/14/05	12:42 am	—	Direct	12/03/05	9:22 pm
Saturn	℞	11/22/05	4:01 am	—	Direct	04/05/06	8:54 am
Venus	℞	12/24/05	4:36 am	—	Direct	02/03/06	4:18 am

Set in Eastern Time. All times corrected for Daylight Saving Time.

Moon Void-of-Course Data for 2005

Last Aspect Date Time	New Sign Sign New Time	Last Aspect Date Time	New Sign Sign New Time	Last Aspect Date Time	New Sign Sign New Time

JANUARY

Last Aspect		New Sign	
2	1:23 am	2 ♎	11:19 am
4	9:20 am	4 ♏	7:00 pm
6	1:29 am	6 ♐	10:44 pm
8	10:02 pm	8 ♑	11:11 pm
10	12:58 am	10 ♒	10:07 pm
12	10:44 am	13 ♓	9:50 pm
14	3:22 am	15 ♈	12:27 am
17	1:57 am	17 ♉	7:06 am
19	5:19 am	19 ♊	5:24 pm
21	4:26 pm	22 ♋	5:42 am
24	4:17 am	24 ♌	6:21 pm
26	5:39 am	27 ♍	6:24 am
29	4:07 pm	29 ♎	5:13 pm
31	10:21 pm	2/1 ♏	1:51 am

FEBRUARY

Last Aspect		New Sign	
1/31	10:21 pm	1 ♏	1:51 am
2	5:56 pm	3 ♐	7:21 am
5	8:07 am	5 ♑	9:32 am
6	8:47 pm	7 ♒	9:26 am
8	11:19 pm	9 ♓	8:59 am
11	12:14 am	11 ♈	10:21 am
13	5:53 am	13 ♉	3:18 pm
15	10:07 pm	16 ♊	12:18 am
18	12:23 am	18 ♋	12:13 pm
20	7:06 am	21 ♌	12:54 am
23	4:47 am	23 ♍	12:44 pm
25	12:00 pm	25 ♎	10:59 pm
27	8:49 pm	28 ♏	7:21 am

MARCH

Last Aspect		New Sign	
2	5:25 am	2 ♐	1:29 pm
4	4:45 am	4 ♑	5:12 pm
6	3:28 am	6 ♒	6:49 pm
8	10:28 am	8 ♓	7:32 pm
10	11:44 am	10 ♈	9:03 pm
12	3:13 pm	13 ♉	1:05 am
15	1:10 am	15 ♊	8:44 am
17	2:19 pm	17 ♋	7:44 pm
20	7:59 am	20 ♌	8:17 am
22	9:20 am	22 ♍	8:10 pm
24	7:36 pm	25 ♎	6:00 am
27	1:29 pm	27 ♏	1:29 pm
29	2:06 am	29 ♐	6:56 pm
31	1:24 pm	31 ♑	10:48 pm

APRIL

Last Aspect		New Sign	
2	9:34 am	3 ♒	1:31 am
4	7:32 pm	5 ♓	4:45 am
6	10:03 pm	7 ♈	7:28 am
9	2:00 am	9 ♉	11:50 am
11	1:37 am	11 ♊	6:55 pm
14	1:01 am	14 ♋	5:03 am
16	10:37 am	16 ♌	5:17 pm
19	4:13 am	19 ♍	5:27 am
21	4:45 am	21 ♎	3:27 pm
23	12:46 pm	23 ♏	10:25 pm
25	8:24 pm	26 ♐	2:46 am
28	2:02 am	28 ♑	5:33 am
29	6:00 pm	30 ♒	7:54 am

MAY

Last Aspect		New Sign	
2	12:47 am	2 ♓	10:43 am
4	4:22 am	4 ♈	2:36 pm
6	9:22 am	6 ♉	8:01 pm
9	1:15 am	9 ♊	3:29 am
11	10:58 am	11 ♋	1:20 pm
13	11:04 am	14 ♌	1:17 am
16	4:57 am	16 ♍	1:46 pm
18	9:00 pm	19 ♎	12:30 am
20	8:40 pm	21 ♏	7:49 am
23	12:54 am	23 ♐	11:38 am
25	2:52 am	25 ♑	1:11 pm
27	11:22 am	27 ♒	2:10 pm
29	5:19 am	29 ♓	4:09 pm
31	1:53 pm	31 ♈	8:07 pm

JUNE

Last Aspect		New Sign	
3	1:24 am	2 ♉	2:20 am
5	1:25 am	5 ♊	10:36 am
7	2:50 pm	7 ♋	8:46 pm
10	6:18 am	10 ♌	8:39 am
12	7:40 am	12 ♍	9:22 pm
15	1:24 am	15 ♎	8:59 am
17	11:02 am	17 ♏	5:23 pm
19	4:06 pm	19 ♐	9:45 pm
21	11:34 am	21 ♑	10:52 pm
23	6:04 pm	23 ♒	10:36 pm
25	11:23 am	25 ♓	11:03 pm
28	1:51 am	28 ♈	1:51 am
30	3:57 am	30 ♉	7:45 am

JULY

Last Aspect		New Sign	
1	1:02 pm	2 ♊	4:26 pm
4	12:36 pm	5 ♋	3:07 am
7	12:54 pm	7 ♌	3:11 pm
9	12:49 pm	10 ♍	3:57 am
12	3:12 pm	12 ♎	4:09 pm
15	1:32 am	15 ♏	1:51 am
16	10:15 am	17 ♐	7:35 am
19	2:03 am	19 ♑	9:26 am
21	7:00 am	21 ♒	8:55 am
23	3:33 am	23 ♓	8:12 am
24	8:19 pm	25 ♈	9:23 am
27	1:23 pm	27 ♉	1:54 pm
29	12:59 am	29 ♊	10:02 pm
31	5:10 pm	8/1 ♋	8:52 am

AUGUST

Last Aspect		New Sign	
7/31	5:10 pm	1 ♋	8:52 am
2	11:59 am	3 ♌	9:10 pm
5	5:45 pm	6 ♍	9:54 am
8	6:10 am	8 ♎	10:08 pm
10	5:10 pm	11 ♏	8:35 am
13	8:06 am	13 ♐	3:47 pm
15	4:43 pm	15 ♑	7:13 pm
16	9:02 pm	17 ♒	7:39 pm
19	1:53 pm	19 ♓	6:52 pm
21	5:45 am	21 ♈	7:01 pm
23	7:46 am	23 ♉	9:58 pm
25	2:14 am	26 ♊	4:43 am
27	10:49 pm	28 ♋	2:57 pm
30	3:22 am	31 ♌	3:14 am

SEPTEMBER

Last Aspect		New Sign	
2	7:44 am	2 ♍	3:56 pm
4	11:40 am	5 ♎	3:52 am
7	4:33 pm	7 ♏	2:10 pm
9	3:31 am	9 ♐	10:03 pm
11	12:52 pm	12 ♑	2:56 am
13	2:22 pm	14 ♒	5:02 am
15	4:23 pm	16 ♓	5:24 am
17	10:01 pm	18 ♈	5:43 am
19	6:36 pm	20 ♉	7:47 am
22	12:41 pm	22 ♊	1:07 pm
24	8:57 am	24 ♋	10:10 pm
26	9:24 pm	27 ♌	10:03 am
29	11:12 am	29 ♍	10:44 pm

OCTOBER

Last Aspect		New Sign	
1	9:22 pm	2 ♎	6:28 am
4	11:15 am	4 ♏	8:03 pm
7	1:51 am	7 ♐	3:28 am
9	2:20 am	9 ♑	8:43 am
11	6:42 am	11 ♒	12:05 pm
13	9:34 am	13 ♓	2:05 pm
15	2:55 am	15 ♈	3:39 pm
17	2:58 pm	17 ♉	6:04 pm
19	6:50 am	19 ♊	10:44 pm
22	5:07 am	22 ♋	6:41 am
24	5:16 pm	24 ♌	5:48 pm
26	10:23 pm	27 ♍	6:28 am
29	5:06 pm	29 ♎	6:15 pm
31	6:17 pm	11/1 ♏	2:29 am

NOVEMBER

Last Aspect		New Sign	
10/31	6:17 pm	1 ♏	2:29 am
2	9:05 am	3 ♐	8:55 am
5	12:58 am	5 ♑	1:17 pm
6	3:18 pm	7 ♒	4:31 pm
9	7:31 am	9 ♓	7:22 pm
11	10:33 am	11 ♈	10:22 pm
13	2:07 pm	14 ♉	2:02 am
15	7:58 pm	16 ♊	7:10 am
18	2:02 am	18 ♋	2:42 pm
20	11:03 pm	21 ♌	1:10 am
23	12:25 am	23 ♍	1:41 pm
25	1:10 pm	26 ♎	1:58 am
27	11:38 pm	28 ♏	11:33 am
30	10:16 am	30 ♐	5:32 pm

DECEMBER

Last Aspect		New Sign	
2	10:17 am	2 ♑	8:42 pm
4	1:56 pm	4 ♒	10:36 pm
6	4:58 pm	7 ♓	12:44 am
8	11:16 pm	9 ♈	4:02 am
11	5:50 am	11 ♉	8:46 am
13	1:46 pm	13 ♊	2:59 pm
15	12:11 pm	15 ♋	11:01 pm
16	7:33 pm	18 ♌	9:18 am
20	8:09 pm	20 ♍	9:39 pm
22	11:30 pm	23 ♎	10:26 am
25	10:53 pm	25 ♏	9:04 pm
27	2:26 am	28 ♐	3:43 am
29	10:01 pm	30 ♑	6:35 am
31	4:09 am	1/1 ♒	?:?? am

Name:

Address, City, State, Zip:

Home Phone: Office Phone:

E-mail: Birthday:

Name:

Address, City, State, Zip:

Home Phone: Office Phone:

E-mail: Birthday:

Name:

Address, City, State, Zip:

Home Phone: Office Phone:

E-mail: Birthday:

Name:

Address, City, State, Zip:

Home Phone: Office Phone:

E-mail: Birthday:

Name:

Address, City, State, Zip:

Home Phone: Office Phone:

E-mail: Birthday:

Name:

Address, City, State, Zip:

Home Phone: Office Phone:

E-mail: Birthday:

Name:

Address, City, State, Zip:

Home Phone: Office Phone:

E-mail: Birthday:

Name:

Address, City, State, Zip:

Home Phone: Office Phone:

E-mail: Birthday:

Name:

Address, City, State, Zip:

Home Phone: Office Phone:

E-mail: Birthday:

Name:

Address, City, State, Zip:

Home Phone: Office Phone:

E-mail: Birthday:

Name:

Address, City, State, Zip:

Home Phone: Office Phone:

E-mail: Birthday:

Name:

Address, City, State, Zip:

Home Phone: Office Phone:

E-mail: Birthday:

Name:

Address, City, State, Zip:

Home Phone: Office Phone:

E-mail: Birthday:

Name:

Address, City, State, Zip:

Home Phone: Office Phone:

E-mail: Birthday:

Name:

Address, City, State, Zip:

Home Phone: Office Phone:

E-mail: Birthday:

Name:

Address, City, State, Zip:

Home Phone: Office Phone:

E-mail: Birthday:

Name:

Address, City, State, Zip:

Home Phone: Office Phone:

E-mail: Birthday:

Name:

Address, City, State, Zip:

Home Phone: Office Phone:

E-mail: Birthday:

Name:

Address, City, State, Zip:

Home Phone: Office Phone:

E-mail: Birthday:

Name:

Address, City, State, Zip:

Home Phone: Office Phone:

E-mail: Birthday:

Name:

Address, City, State, Zip:

Home Phone: Office Phone:

E-mail: Birthday:

Name:

Address, City, State, Zip:

Home Phone: Office Phone:

E-mail: Birthday:

Name:

Address, City, State, Zip:

Home Phone: Office Phone:

E-mail: Birthday:

Name:

Address, City, State, Zip:

Home Phone: Office Phone:

E-mail: Birthday:

Name:

Address, City, State, Zip:

Home Phone: Office Phone:

E-mail: Birthday:

Name:

Address, City, State, Zip:

Home Phone: Office Phone:

E-mail: Birthday:

Name:

Address, City, State, Zip:

Home Phone: Office Phone:

E-mail: Birthday:

Name:

Address, City, State, Zip:

Home Phone: Office Phone:

E-mail: Birthday:

Name:

Address, City, State, Zip:

Home Phone: Office Phone:

E-mail: Birthday:

Name:

Address, City, State, Zip:

Home Phone: Office Phone:

E-mail: Birthday: